Dare to be
your Master

Diseño de portada: Editorial Sirio, S.A.

© de la edición original
2013 Suzanne Powell

© de la presente edición
EDITORIAL SIRIO, S.A.

EDITORIAL SIRIO, S.A.
C/ Rosa de los Vientos, 64
Pol. Ind. El Viso
29006-Málaga
España

www.editorialsirio.com
sirio@editorialsirio.com

I.S.B.N.: 978-84-16233-86-1
Depósito Legal: MA-1178-2015

Printed in Spain

SUZANNE POWELL

Dare to be
your Master

editorial Sirio

The greater one's personal evolution,
The more like a child one becomes.

Enrique Barrios
Ami: Child of the Stars

This book is dedicated to my dear mother, Joy Powell, who at the age of seventy five recovered from a life-threatening experience which lasted four days, during which the idea for this book was conceived. I thank her for having chosen to continue amongst us, sharing so much fun and love. She always has been, and always will be a great source of inspiration for me. I hope to be able to give her personally a copy of the book, signed in gratitude for these 50 years together.

Infinite thanks.
I love you beyond time and space.

Prologue

I must confess that when I became interested in reading as a teenager, more often than not, I skipped the prologue. Of course, patience was not one of my greatest virtues at that time. As I began to understand that writing was something really fascinating, and that reading was a wonderful way of finding out about other human beings and being able to experience the contrasts and beauty of this planet, something in me changed. It was then that I started to appreciate the work involved in relating a story or an event, whether it be short or long, or have anything to do with us or not. Finding the words that move others deeply, looking for someone to publish them, the discouragement that goes along with hearing the same thing over and over again, why you are writing, what is the purpose of it... Gradually, I began to appreciate each and every detail of a book, from the colour of the cover, to the depth of its words, and from their subtle correctness to the very author who interlaces each of the paragraphs in order to show us something that he or she has learnt, whether we like it or not.

If anyone had told me twenty years ago that one day Suzannne Powell would offer me the opportunity of writing a prologue and being part of one of her books, I would have merely considered it as a wild fantasy.

But, as you can see, even the least suspected fantasy can become true. Even the dreams that we deem highly improbable can be fulfilled. Why do we so often think "no"...!

Dare to be your Master is a fitting title. And what is more surprising, it is amazingly clear. However, take my advice; this book is to be read with heartfelt energy and devotion, because it is not exactly a simplistic approach to happiness.

It is an uncomplicated invitation to feel joyful. A celebration of who we are and our magnificent ability. A vote of confidence that we give ourselves; for once, and hopefully more and more from now on, opt to leave your mind behind, because when you read Suzanne's words, you will not take long in remembering that the mind is only part of us, that in no way, shape or form does it define us, regardless of how much you have been led to think so, and that it never will.

I am sure that when you finish reading this book, you will ask yourself the same question I asked myself: how much longer are we going to waste time not being real people? People who accept the lessons they set themselves, who do not fear the consequences of being themselves, who withdraw from the dependence which generates victimisation, who recognise the illusion of fear. Is it not ridiculous that we dare not even pursue a dream or a life project?

Look around you, search carefully in your memory and you will discover just how many of those "grown-ups" who surround us declare that they stopped dreaming a long time ago or that you cannot expect any more from life and that life is just that. They even make us regard with shame the word "childish". So many opportunities have passed us by, through not treasuring and appreciating our own experience, but simply following someone else who seems more perfect, more sublime, more advanced than ourselves.

In addition, paragraph by paragraph, Suzanne dares in many ways to expose parts of her own life, showing us how each and every human being can learn to master the inner self. We all have this right, and this magnificent ability. She opens the door on some of her personal experiences so that we may recognise ourselves in the same contradictory and difficult situations. She encourages us to abandon the delusion of the unattainable, and to engage a sense of humour in this school of learning called Life. Furthermore, I have a feeling that any reflection you may have on savouring her words will leave you quickly imbued. Her strategy is basic yet essential: stop trying and just do it.

The language of Suzanne's book is calm and colloquial. Many of those who are drawn by splendour would not accept it as noteworthy quality; however, the intimacy of her expressions, those sentences composed from the heart, all reveal to us something very important: spirituality is not only compatible with simplicity but is marvellously suited to a good sense of humour.

Dare to be your Master is not an instructions manual on metaphysics, nor is it an exhaustive list of advice for the soul but embodies a generous sharing of much personal learning, which humbly invites us to become more aware. Those of you who know the writer will smile at the following words: "If I can, you can".

Suzanne is a valuable travelling companion who constantly opens the doors which we never cease to close. I know how much care and good will have gone into the writing of this book. Believe me when I assure you that her words are full of both excitement and protection. You yourselves will sense it from the very first page and far from leaving you disappointed, each chapter will provide you with greater feeling. Surrender yourselves openly to these feelings, for all you are worth.

Finally, using the same words that the writer uses on numerous occasions, proceed to read with an open mind, an open heart and open hands. The time has come to nurture the master who lies dormant in the interior of each and every one of us.

ISABEL SIMÓN
Author of the book of short stories *Algunos como yo*
And coauthor of *Desoladas*
Founder of the literary creative
and critic blog, *«Exdesoladas»*
And cofounder of the *Tertulia Literaria Café Ajenjo.*
Madrid, August 2013

Foreword

Victoria-Palace Hotel, El Escorial, Spain, 15-18 April 2013.

(This book is the product of a channeling carried out in fifteen hours over four days. It constitutes a transcription in real time with a subsequent adaptation into text form.)

What is the point of exploring self-mastery at this moment? Why is everyone talking about this now?

Not so long ago, I was in a profound state of relaxation. Ahead of me were four free days while my daughter was away on a school trip with friends. Bearing in mind these four days, I decided not to deal with any consultations and allow things to take their course, without making any plans, without arranging to meet anyone, seeing as programming just a week of my life is a long term project. Deep inside, I knew that there was something outstanding, something that I had to share, and I was waiting for that moment of disconnection from my routine to find out what it could be. I needed that break.

I must confess that many ideas came to mind. One of which was to catch a plane and go off to a paradise island and enjoy the warmth after a long winter in Madrid. But that idea came and went. I also considered the possibility of going on a retreat to a Buddhist monastery with a friend of mine. But that idea also vanished. I even thought of visiting my parents in Ireland. But that idea too quickly disappeared. Until one morning, while I was having a bath, and very relaxed, I felt the need to find a quiet space, near the mountains and away from the noise of the city, and invite a friend to share the break. It was in this way that this book took shape in just four days.

My Self wisely knew that Xavi, my friend, would be more than ready to cooperate. And so it was: without a doubt, he agreed happily to be my transcriber. We decided to make the most of the opportunity as a gift, as an offering, with joy and enthusiasm, to write *Dare to be your Master*. I thank you for that, Xavi.

Recalculating, recalculating... My transcriber was going on holiday for almost forty days to celebrate his fortieth birthday, but he recalculated. Also, effortlessly... Four days on holiday together? No, four days working on the text, fulfilling our intention to pool all that we could.

Introduction

I received the information that I was to write this book via a channeling which I experienced on the last day of the great Mayan cycle: 21st December 2012. The idea rang clear inside me: "You will write a book with this title".

My first reaction was to ask myself why I should undertake this assignment when I was still learning to be the master of my Self. But I was captivated by the title and I felt it was necessary to be daring, because in actual fact, nobody teaches us how to become a master. That is why one of our greatest tasks in life revolves around learning to be the master of our Self and to share, generously, all that we have learnt.

It is like when a couple have their first-born child. They ask themselves: "Where is the instruction booklet? How will this new being know what to do? And what about us parents?" The answer is simple: we all learn as we go along. And at each moment, we ask ourselves: "Are we doing things right?

As if by magic, your child accepts everything. Whether you are doing things right or wrong is not important for him. He simply accepts your nature as a father or a mother. When we find ourselves in the process of self-mastery, it does not matter how we do it. We are called upon to be the master of our Self. Whether we want to or not, every personal experience will help us to gain mastery in everything we do.

Everything in life serves as a lesson.
Experience nourishes us, filling us with life and wisdom.

With greater or lesser fluency, we learn from the situations that life puts in front of us. Depending on our level of personal development, we live these experiences as human beings, either with confusion or with clarity, at times in ignorance and at others in wisdom. One of the best ways to learn is by means of reflection. You can listen to many opinions and heed their advice or ignore them, though sooner or later you will inevitably realise that in some way, everything is perfect just as it is, everything is fine, it always has been and it always will be. You start to be aware of the existence of a greater order where everything has a reasonable explanation, which at times we are unaware of and which we may find difficult to understand right now. But everything is fine. Everything flows towards a common good, and this is a great lesson in self-mastery.

Thanks to reflection, we learn that we are a kind of human GPS, (Global Positioning System), like radars that detect the signs and we begin to direct our lives in a different direction. Whatever the outcome, we are ready to change at any moment, and pursue our path of life towards something greater and more profound, which is more authentic and joyful. Despite what our relatives, friends and boss might say, or even our own thoughts, we become more and more ready to go one step further along the path of inner experience, that of a true spiritual approach towards connecting with the most divine part of our being.

> When you surrender to your multi-dimensional being, and you allow your Self to be, it is then that you become a complete human being, full of joy and great spiritual serenity.

This calmness is borne from the innocence of a small child and the wisdom of an old man. At times, this new way of seeing and feeling life does not fit in with the world around us, but that also forms part of the challenge of awakening to this flow of consciousness. On awakening to self-mastery, we must inevitably break free from old patterns and systems of thought which are no more than former ways of seeing and understanding the world. As we proceed to do this, others will do so too.

The secret lies in knowing how to live this new presence while being ourselves yet assuming all the consequences; how to be constantly here in the now, aware and present in everything we do and think and in every feeling which emerges from within us every second of our lives. My favourite mantra could well be: "What difference does it make!"

That is what I mean when I talk about spiritual calm. What difference does it make! Everything is fine. Living like this, I can laugh at myself, getting in touch with my inner child, trying to identify with neither my own emotional and psychological dramas, nor anybody else's. When this is the case, we no longer want to sap the life out of anyone or for anyone else to bleed us dry. Once we reach this state, our sole desire is to share the experience of abundance we are now living. The abundance of our Being.

We must observe with impartiality any kind of conflict which appears, without dramatising. Seen from the outside, everything changes. If you choose happiness, harmony, peace, innocence... you relax in all aspects and find yourself living in a state of tranquillity which becomes your favourite swimming pool, a lake of personal strength. You cease to live in the turbulent waters of a stormy, volatile sea. Even though you may see a threatening wave, you know that once it reaches the shore, it will be lulled, with no fear of it reaching you or affecting you, because everything continues to pass, everything returns to the sea, to the ocean. It is wonderful to accept oneself and fearlessly say: "I am as I am", like it or not; this is my story, my song, my life and I choose to be happy being like this, accepting myself, embracing myself and being at peace with every part of me.

This works for me. And everyone should find what works for him or her to discover who they are, to fulfil their lives and to listen to their inner voice. And from then on, they will realise their purpose, their mission on this planet, in this world, at each and every instant.

To get where I am now, accepting myself as I am, I have undergone many conflictive incidents; highly dramatized moments of victimisation, annoyance and tedium, although deep down I always knew that everything would turn out for the best. In fact, everything works out right if we simply allow the natural flow of the universal laws.

The Law of Attraction, the Law of Polarity, the Law of Compensation, the Law of Karma –otherwise known as the law of cause and effect– they all lead us towards harmony. As they say in the East: "He who cries a lot shall also laugh a lot."

We must learn to be aware of our words, thoughts and deeds. We learn as we go along. We have no instruction booklet. We choose to live and experience life, just like the captain of a ship navigates through the storm, hand at the helm, knowing that sooner or later, come what may, he will safely arrive home. Arriving home is living the fulfilling life we are worthy of, full of peace and love, dedication and service, support and mutual help; the life of a complete human being.

The human GPS guides our lives and adjusts at each moment to what must happen. To use my favourite words: "Our human GPS is recalculating."

We are changing cycles, and therefore, adjusting our frequency to a new wave length. It is as if we have changed from a three star hotel to a five star without moving from where we are. We know that there are changes that we can feel, even touch; even though we are seeing the same furniture and walls, we sense that something has changed. There are now bathrobes, slippers and perhaps even a sauna in this new dimension. There is an improvement in everything around us, on this more sophisticated, beautiful frequency that is new to us. SELF-MASTERY HELPS US TO SEE THROUGH NEW EYES ALL THAT SURROUNDS US. It encourages us to pay more attention to the simple things in life, the beautiful manifestation of Nature. We spend more time contemplating fields, valleys, rivers and flowers, truly enjoying a walk or a child's smile. We begin to transform our ordinary life into something quite extraordinary, with deeper meaning. Even washing the dishes is no longer the tedious, mechanical chore of washing the dishes but an opportunity to feel the water flowing through our fingers and appreciate the freshness of the moisture. We can redesign each moment from a much more authentic and beautiful perspective. Having changed status, there are new laws, and new guidelines which tell you: "Whatever you need, just ask for it". Now when we ask, we receive. We have paid a high price to reach this new frequency, this new place, and we deserve, by the Law of Compensation, to receive what we have paid for.

The Law of Compensation brings us what is ours.

When we mentally make plans and have a clear idea of what we want, we aim in that direction without becoming obsessed with the outcome; instead we go with the flow, feeling happy and enthusiastic about our target, about our objective. The mind may have a thousand clear ideas and if we surrender to our Self to live a greater experience, all circumstances adjust so that those ideas come in to being. The mind may resist, protesting over the changes, but we must learn to accept the new circumstances, telling ourselves: "Recalculating, recalculating, recalculating", knowing that this unexpected change has occurred because there is something even better awaiting us.

Relax. It is a matter of being relaxed. If doubt arises from inner confusion and conflict, we must calm down. We must remain tranquil. Bear in mind that we cannot see the answers when we enter a state of anxiety, confusion or fear. We must look within and patiently ask ourselves what is the best solution. It is important to maintain an even keel in the face of any challenge. Only by controlling our emotions, remaining calm and serene, can we choose. We sit down, we take a deep breath and we ask ourselves: "What is the best solution?" And from this state of stillness it is easy to find the answer. If it does not surface at that very moment, we simply move on and occupy ourselves with something or other, and when we least expect it, the perfect idea, the precise answer, the divine inspiration will occur to us. AS A MATTER OF FACT, FOR EVERY PROBLEM THAT WE MAY ENCOUNTER, THERE ARE AT LEAST TEN SOLUTIONS. We just need to pay attention and know how to decipher the signs, notifications and messages hidden in each present reality.

Awakening

What is the meaning of awakening? It is merely to shift from a state of ignorance to that of understanding life from a different, broader and deeper perspective.

From the moment I was born, I felt something was different. While I was at school, I would watch my classmates, observe my teachers, and could not stop thinking: "Don't they realise that there's something else. Don't they know that some people are special?" I remember being at school at the age of six or seven and hiding away to cry to myself because I felt deep inside that I did not belong there. A feeling of loneliness weighed me down while I listened to the teacher in class who seemed miles away. Absorbed in a cloud, floating, being without really being. I often recalled the image of my father's face when he used to leave me at the school gates and feeling just how much I loved him. I continued in much the same manner, growing up and working my way through school as a star pupil – luckily, I achieved high grades in all my subjects. I had my friends and just tried to be a normal girl, just a plain Jane. I wanted to be like everyone else. At home, I was the elder sister, and inevitably shouldered the responsibility of being like a second mother for my brothers and sisters. Always with that feeling of being different, as if I did not really belong to that family, as if I was just performing a role. But deep down, I wanted to get out of there, to fly, to feel alive and experience life. I wanted to be seen for who I was.

I remember how my father used to tell me: "Whatever you do, don't go into teaching." I had always admired him because he was an eminent teacher. Perhaps due to that, I ended up studying Romance Languages and Literature and I ventured into the world of education. In fact, the first nine years that I spent in Spain, I worked as a teacher. However, I swore to myself to never to become the teacher stereotype that I had come across up until then. I wanted to be different. I wanted to leave an impression on my students so that they would remember me for being a good teacher who had given them something besides knowledge. In actual fact, they were my first masters. I talked like they did, laughed like they did and even dressed the same as they did. I listened to their feelings of dissatisfaction, grief and joy as an equal. We did things together and enjoyed ourselves.

I can still remember the looks on their faces when I would arrive at the classroom. I loved their expressions of enthusiasm and curiosity, of expectation and delight about what they were to learn that particular day. I honestly believe I had managed to touch their hearts. Those classes portrayed soul learnt lessons, teachings that I wanted to convey to make them happy. I TAUGHT THEM HOW TO LISTEN TO THEMSELVES SO THAT EACH COULD DISCOVER HIS OR HER OWN TALENT, OR GIFT, REGARDLESS OF ANY SOCIAL OR FAMILY OPINION. First of all, they had to be happy and to express themselves freely.

After those first years, I left the school to enter the field of nutrition. I had a new public to conquer: naturopaths, doctors, herbalists... Initiating myself in this new domain gave me the chance to expand my own knowledge, travel to many different countries and come into contact with outstanding professionals in the world of nutrition and orthomolecular research. I found it all very fascinating. My life revolved around reading, searching, experimenting.

DURING THAT PERIOD I BEGAN TO BE THE MASTER OF MY OWN BODY. After enduring a transformation in my physical and mental well-being – I overcame several digestive problems, many allergies and cancer – the experience motivated me to offer my own accomplishment in order to help others to regain their health. At the same time, I learnt from the experiences of others. Thanks to this new learning, I learnt to listen to my body and to find my own balance, in terms of my nervous system, immune system and digestive system. I successfully achieved a balance based on this new skill of mastery. However, it was not enough. It lacked something. I was tuning in to a holistic approach, the body and mind from a different angle. "But what about the spirit?" My spirit felt starved and also wanted to grow and develop. My mind was full of existential questions like: "Who am I? What am I doing here? Am I a human being that's been hurled onto this planet along with millions of other beings? Why? Where do we all come from and where are we going?" I recall the hours

I spent contemplating the stars, asking myself day in, day out: "Why do I feel so alone? Why doesn't anyone come and find me? Why isn't there any love? Why is there so much suffering in the world? Where is my family? Why do I feel sad? Where this thing is called unconditional love? I have no reason to feel like this; I'm healthy, I've got money, a home... Why do I feel as if something's missing when I've got so much to be grateful for?" All this lamenting and yearning is just what put me on the right road towards spiritual growth. I reckoned: "If I don't ask myself these questions, how will I ever find the answers?" And for that reason, I would wake up every day with the same doubts: "Who am I? What am I doing here? I want to know why. I need to know, I want to know."

This calling was answered with a wonderful experience which I enjoyed after making the acquaintance of someone who later became my master during his lifetime. By his side, thanks to his infinite generosity, I learnt a precious teaching which is totally soul-fulfilling, a valuable tool which I continue to use as it serves to help so many other people. Every single day, I thank the Universe for giving me the opportunity to share this wonderful gift with everyone.

When this master passed away, I felt alone again, as if abandoned by life. I was repeatedly assailed by thoughts of this nature: "Who will understand me now when he actually understood me almost better than myself?" I often recalled how he used to tell me that he was not my master, even though he allowed me to call him as such. With infinite patience, he helped me realise that I was my own master and that everyone had to take control of their own life and practise self-mastery. He was simply a guide.

I remember how good it was to feel in his presence and how fulfilled I used to feel on hearing his words of wisdom. Until the moment arrived when I understood that I did not need him near me to feel the same way. Sometime later, I was woken up one day in my bed by a marvellous experience: I was in a tunnel and I suddenly collided with a great luminous energy which penetrated my forehead and merged with me. It was as if I had become that very light, with immense pleasure in my soul, unified with Totality, joyful and ecstatic; yes, pure cosmic ecstasy. It was at that moment that I awoke. I understood all that I had not understood up until now in my life. I suddenly began to laugh because I realised that we are doing everything the wrong way round. WE DO NOT HAVE TO TRY TO DO ANYTHING. Everything is fine, just as it is. Nobody is at fault. Each and every one of us is carrying out a process that we ourselves designed, with no need to label things right or wrong. Everything is, everything just IS. "Wow!!!" I reflected.

But when my mind tried to interpret what had happened, the experience faded. It was like when the lens of a camera opens and closes in a split second. The fact that I did not remember what had happened to me was not important; being bombarded by so much information was what awoke me from my stupor. In that precise instant, I could truly say: "I now know everything". But just as quickly as it appeared, it was lost. It was a gift from my Self to reassure and calm my heart and mind, not to worry about anything ever again. I was never to be afraid, as I would always be guided. All I had to do was to live the present moment to the full and follow what I felt in my heart. Later, however, I was tormented by a question. "How can I transmit this to my fellow teachers? How can I help them understand that our master did not want to teach us a set of rules and regulations with regard to meditation, conscious breathing and the laying on of hands therapy, but to show us how to be ourselves?"

What I had experienced during that moment was a vision of my Self, free of ego, mind and personality. My soul had opened up, baring my true essence. I now knew what was truly important as I remembered these words: "Open mind, open heart, open hands".

We must always have an open mind,
an open heart and open hands

We have simply been given the tools to calm the pain of our physical body, to regain peace and clarity in our mind and thus to achieve a state of fulfilment and harmony. I understood the true meaning of what I had been taught. However, I felt as if my colleagues were only halfway there, practising a simple hands-on procedure based on inflexible rules and set methods. They had forgotten the essential aspect. Just like when you are about to sign a contract, it is imperative that you read the terms carefully, especially the small print. There is always small print at the end. In life, we receive our diploma but the small print adds: "Use this with an open mind, an open heart and open hands".

Practise and develop through experience, with humility,
simplicity and unconditional love. This is the way of the great.

From the moment my master departed, and with this new understanding, the question I put to the universe was this: "If I have briefly experienced the act of awakening, if I have humbly managed to savour a moment of clarity, a split second of insight, how can I share this so that others too are able to live their own experience and also awaken?" When Jesus said: "I am the way. Follow me", he did not mean it literally. He just wanted to say: "Take my example. Do as I do". That is why I insist over and over again at my conferences: "If others have been able, you can too". We all have the potential to attain self-mastery. We just need to follow the example of those who have succeeded or are in the process of doing so. It is just a case of imitating those actions and values which work and which serve to promote the well-being of mankind progressing towards a better world. Jesus professed: "You will do greater things".

It was then that I sensed that life had plans for me. I wondered how I could help others to live their own experience, based on the insight from my own.

The man from the mountain

One day, in Ciudatella Park, Barcelona I was walking around the fair being held in celebration of Earth Day and while my daughter was having her face painted at one of the craft stalls, a rather strange-looking man appeared out of nowhere. He was about sixty years old with the air of a vagabond. He wore shabby clothes — a worn out leather jacket and a pair of jeans much in need of washing — and a coloured cap on his head. He had a long white beard and his hair was tied back in a pony-tail. He approached me and said to me in a deep masculine voice:

"Madam, I've spent the last eight years looking for you and even though I don't like coming here, to this city of cement, I've undergone this journey to find you and your daughter. By the way, where is your daughter?

I do not recall the look on my face at that moment but I assumed that this man was confused and had mistaken me with someone else. But then my daughter turned up and he opened his arms wide to greet her as if he had known her all her life.

He asked me to help him with a job that he wanted to do the following day in Güell Park. He asked me to be there at twelve o'clock mid-day. My judgemental mind was telling me: "There's no way I'm going with this man, looking like he does, to do a job". My mind simply shut down, causing a negative reaction to the proposal.

"Let me think it over tonight", I offered.

To this he answered: "I knew you'd say that, Madam. I've heard they call you 'Miss Confirmation'. Think it over all you want, but tomorrow we'll meet at twelve". I was struck by his determination. This gave all the more reason to meditate and speak with my master about this new adventure. The response was conclusive: "Just do it!" I sighed. "What was I getting myself into?" Nevertheless, I remembered something my master had told me some years previously: "Don't be surprised in the future if a beggar appears and gives you orders, because EVEN A BEGGAR COULD BE AN ENLIGHTENED BEING IN DISGUISE. DO NOT JUDGE ANYONE BY THEIR APPEARANCE".

So, at twelve o'clock on the dot, I arrived at my appointment with my daughter and a couple of friends in order to feel less vulnerable. The man beat his drum while my daughter and I stood listening, meditating with one eye shut and the other one open, not knowing what could happen. Later, he led us to a fountain and talked to us about the river of life. He took out a crystal, put it in the water and performed a ritual which we did not understand. All the time, I tried to maintain a receptive attitude, at least to accept this new experience as another opportunity to learn. I must admit that I was captivated. Afterwards, we talked for a long time. I listened attentively trying not to judge, but staying apart from my mind and opening my soul to the positivity of that moment. Paying attention, curious to know what he had to tell me, I realised that I was in the presence of a wise man, someone who had appeared at that moment because I had to learn from him. At the end of that exceptional day, he asked us to visit his home in the mountains of Teruel (Spain) and spend the May bank holiday weekend with him there. After meditating on what had happened and his request, and of course, having received confirmation, we decided to accept his invitation.

At a later date, I underwent another experience in which I flew out of my body to a kind of room where I could watch my own life programme. I saw a great maze where a lot of people appeared; some I knew and some I did not. I also saw a kind of staircase with steps and walls which I had to jump onto to reach the next step. I was aware that this represented my personal progress. I could see my path and the possible distractions in the labyrinth of life. The staircase stretched from one point to another. I realised that I, my-self, had designed that journey and therefore was free to fo-llow it straight ahead or become distracted in the maze along the way. I was glad to be able to understand the game and grasp the concept so expansively. Overcome with happiness, I knew that everything is worthwhile in order to arrive at the finish. Being able to contemplate the whole game, the com-plete interplay, gave me a feeling of confidence. It is when you begin to understand that you enter fully into the game because you know everything will turn out fine and be wor-thwhile, and that everything will be perfect. You start to live life from a different viewpoint. In short, it is a game, a sta-ge play where you sense your whole existence with extreme intensity.

I came to the conclusion that the 'man from the moun-tain' had helped me to learn to love another being that was distinct from me, with different clothing to mine, and com-pletely opposite to me in his approach to interpreting life, a life that I had mentally encoded in terms of judgement and prejudice. It was a total surprise when I arrived at his house, and he greeted me with arms open wide, saying: "Welcome to the fifth dimension".

Even greater was my surprise when I saw the portrait of my master hanging on the wall of his 'shack'. And even more surprising was when my daughter, who was five years old at the time, gave him a drawing of three mountains with two suns, one of which had thought bubbles. I remember thin-king that one of the suns had ears and when I asked her why, my daughter said: "They aren't ears, they're thoughts. That sun is you and the other one is the man from the mountain.

You've got ears because you don't know what to do. 'Should I go or shouldn't I? Yes? No?' That's why you've got thought bubbles – ears full of thoughts!"

In the drawing, there was a square containing the word 'mint'. The man from the mountain burst out laughing on seeing it. Then he told me: "Madam, look behind you". Right there behind me was a box of freshly cut mint. Then he added: "Your daughter comes here every night to play with the unicorns in the mountains, you know. She made me promise her to prepare some mint tea for you on your arrival. Now has come the time to keep my promise".

By this time, I was well and truly confused so I simply told myself: "Suzanne, go with the flow".

After many long conversations, and having overcome my allergy to cats (there must have been at least twenty), to dust, to mites, to hay... in short, once I had overcome all my weaknesses, I realised that those four days were necessary in order to retrace the steps I had taken, unlearn all that I had learnt and break the code of my mind. A new version of Suzanne had to be born; a new register with a more up-to-date, broader span of prospects.

When I had met this man in Güell Park that day at noon, I remembered him saying to me: "By the way, Madam, last night a master spoke to me delivering this message: ' I entrust you with a mother and her daughter. Do your work and when it's completed, send them home again'".

I received lots of messages throughout those days. I sensed that I was on the right road. I knew I had to free my mind, open my heart and spread my wings. It was time to be myself with all its consequences.

During those days, I learnt how to relate with the incredible world of the elements, the power of Nature, and how to connect with Mother Earth. I withdrew to various parts of the mountains and learnt how to communicate with multidimensional beings. I discovered how to fly in a multidimensional way, began to conceive space and time differently, and could disconnect from my mind one minute to find myself consciously aware on the other side of the Universe just seconds later. I learnt how to link up with my inner hard disk, connect with my own Self and communicate with other people's.

They were four intense days of unforgettable experiences, not just for me, but also for my daughter who enjoyed seeing how the chrysalis revealed a beautiful butterfly. During those days, she looked happy and carefree, far from the commonplace noise of civilisation. I even felt sorry about the kind of upbringing I was giving her in the city. I realised that I could well be wrong, even though I had tried to do my best for her.

At the end of those four magical days, back in Barcelona once again, she would draw huge smiles on our faces, our eyes open wider than ever. I had gained a different perception of existence, a different sensitivity. I watched people in all spheres of life and experienced a great feeling of love towards humanity. The desire arose in me to help people to find themselves, join together, being with being, with open hearts. I felt the need to share my experience of life and I began to look for the way to transmit all that I had learnt and was feeling. And so it was that I gave my first conferences, although they were never made public on Internet because nobody filmed them.

Gradually I opened up, daring to explain my experiences in life. I use the word DARE because this involved being exposed to criticism and disagreement from people who had learned alongside me. It was inevitable. However, I paid little attention seeing as I has been in the same situation as them up until that humble awakening, that broader vision of life. I knew that they were just dormant to that reality, that awareness which I was now enjoying and which one day, they would too enjoy. I had to continue on my journey, with or without them. I spent four years on my own with my daughter, teaching without any kind of assistance. One day, someone from my school of teaching decided to ask me about my own personal experiences. Thanks to their open minds, I could talk to him and his colleagues about my achievement. That is how the word spread. At first, perhaps through curiosity, they began to attend courses but were unable to avert what they were feeling, remembering the old times, when our master gave us classes. Their hearts began to open. They could not refrain from feeling. It was a calling from the soul which told them: "Resume your journey". Due to my testimony, they began to live their own experience.

Even though I had begun my journey in a completely opposite direction to that of my colleagues, some of them were aware that this was the way of the truth. The fact that I had been daring to be myself enabled me to be my own master with all the consequences.

The secret is in taking that step, diving blindly into the swimming pool because something deep down inside of you, your very soul, tells you it is right for you. Somehow, you know just what to do; in spite of what your mind is telling you, you know what your purpose is, and your inner mission too, an impulse you must follow. So I dived in, thus initiating a chain reaction. When you fulfil your purpose with enthusiasm, love and complete and utter conviction, from the very heart of you, with the true essence of your being, you transmit all this to others. Just like an infectious smile which is hard to avoid. You become a kind of beacon, lighting up everything around you, and attracting others, not for you to be their master but for them to awake to their own inner master, their interior light and transparent vision. A vibrational spiral is activated which penetrates everything attracted towards it.

If you feel enthusiastic about your aim, your goal, your purpose in life, become aligned with the complete certainty that this is what you want at this moment. In this way, your intention will implicate itself totally in this experience. This is what happens when the spiral force becomes activated and the Universe gives you more and more of the same thing, although you must keep an open mind and be prepared to change at any moment. Always recalculating and adapting to what is new, because everything is transformed in this cycle of constant change.

Only the present moment exists. An eternal now. It may be that at this present moment you feel like doing something different. We are continuously changing inside. We live a process of constant change. This is the universal principle that keeps everything in motion. Consequently, everything is being modified at every instant. We should do as children do: "Now I want this, now I want that". We scold them for such an arbitrary nature, yet they know perfectly what they want. When we know clearly what we want, we are already on the right track. Everything will be clarified as we proceed and transcend.

> Do not focus on what you do not want, as the Universe will expand it and give you more of what you do not want. The Universe cannot interpret the word 'no'.

The programme

The man from the mountain was very clear about what he wanted. He did not want to be just another number in society, or subjected to the system. Nor did he want to be dependent on anyone. He simply wanted to live. In actual fact, he died twice and came back to life. He experimented with every shade of life, from the darkness of drugs to the brightness of human simplicity. In spite of being labelled as the local madman, people came to him from all over the world to experience moments of awakening. I considered him to be the perfect example of a person who dared to be his own master.

The man from the mountain was already in my programme. I had to go through the experience of meeting him in order to learn how to direct my life and be aware of this. If I understand and accept that I have a predetermined programme, I must respect the fact that each and every other human being has theirs too, and understand that they are all doing exactly what they have to do, according to what they have planned for themselves.

We know that mistakes do not exist; at the most, they may be considered as distractions. Such are the moments when we pause and recalculate our route at a given point. Life is cyclical. That is why lessons appear over and over again in different situations until they are learnt. Once it is learnt, the lesson disappears. During my experience with the man from the mountain I learnt the lesson of Unconditional Love. I also learnt how not to prejudge. I saw how many people who visited him were unable to experience what their soul required at that moment due to mistrust. They would leave no sooner had they arrived. I remember him saying to me: "Thank you, Madam, for keeping an open mind. That makes my work with you so much easier".

When I finally left, he congratulated me: "Well done, Madam. You have passed the test".

It was then that I started to cry.

This episode leads us to the programme, towards our own purpose. Everyone has his own personal programme which also forms part of a collective purpose, in other words, a greater purpose which all those who acquire self-mastery understand and serve wisely in silent detachment.

The programme works like a computer game with many options: "If I do this that might occur, but if I do the other, something different may happen".

We all carry a predetermined programme inside us, packed with extensive options which are also designed according to the lessons or experiences that we must assimilate and learn. This programme, in this lifetime, is only a fraction of the programme of all our life cycles. It functions in the same way as a computer connected to many other computers via a great central exchange, but in this case to an intranet or perhaps even to a cyberspace. Each person directs his or her own programme, whether they are aware of it or not and always affects the collective programme, constantly interacting with it. We are all essential to this universal evolutionary process. Any decision you make on a personal level also affects the collective level. We are all one; we are one unified humanity, although sometimes, when faced with fear and the lack of insight, we feel isolated, disconnected and alone.

How to be the master of oneself

First of all, we must be aware of our thoughts in order to be aware of our words, those all important tools for the cocreation of our lives. Just as you think your life will be, so it will be. If our thoughts are pure and free from prejudice, vibrating on a high frequency and full of enthusiasm, excitement and happiness, our very existence will be equally as pure and positive. When I pronounce a word, this becomes a vibrational energy in terms of behaviour and action, that is to say, something that can be touched, felt and perceived. Words, the same as thoughts, are charged with vibrations. Once they are emitted, they travel outwards, to the Universe and then return to us. Always, yes, ALWAYS. For that reason, we must be aware of the power of words and the power of thoughts. Whatever you say, so shall it be. Needless to say, be careful of what you think and what you say.

The more aware you become of your life, the more conscious you start to be, and the more Zen you are. Knowing what you are thinking, how you are behaving, is to be Zen. Only too often do we create our own hell due to our unawareness. Through not being truly aware of words, we can create conflict or even condition our programming and live in constant suffering.

We often use set phrases without thinking. Consider, for example: "This food is to die for!" "My life's a wreck." "That ice-cream will make you feel sick." Words like these would really grate on anyone who was truly conscious. Think twice before you say those kinds of things. When we use these expressions, we produce a precept which we impose on others and ourselves, given that whatever we wish for others we also wish for ourselves.

That leads me to think of chain e-mails such as: "Send this e-mail to twenty people or you will have bad luck." And to make things worse, you have got to do it in the next twenty minutes. Immediately, the person who receives a message like this thinks: "I'll do it" - just in case it is true. Then, when they have sent the message to twenty people on their contact list, they can sit back and relax, thinking: "Phew! That's a weight off my mind!" But what they have done in actual fact is transmit unease or apprehension to twenty other people – and to thousands of others on the rebound – whether consciously or unconsciously. If someone decides not to forward the e-mail, they may feel guilty for 'breaking the chain' and may even become ill due to it. Who is responsible? If you have participated in any way, shape or form, you must assume your part of responsibility within your programme, and you should know that through that action you have created a debt and karma.

If anyone sends us a chain e-mail, we should neither believe it nor assume any responsibility, other than that of breaking the chain, which may contain beliefs or words that spread fear and harm. I personally send a conscious reply to anyone who sends me one of these e-mails to inform them of what they have just done and at the same time, invite them to take a look at my videos on karma. THE WRITTEN OR SPOKEN WORD HAS THE SAME STRENGTH AS THE THOUGHT BEHIND IT. That is why we must be aware at all times of what we think, say or write. This must be applied to me in two aspects: as a person and as a writer, I must endeavour for everything I write to be of benefit rather than a burden for those who read my work.

Beliefs

From the moment we are born, we accumulate beliefs that have been transmitted, ingrained or even imposed on us. We have chosen these beliefs as our way of thinking, personality and upbringing, depending on what has rung true inside us, not only with regard to religion but to beliefs of any nature.

In fact, in present day society, we get carried away by the beliefs of others; mainly, by those of our own family. We accept the ideals of our parents, grandparents and distant ancestors. We assume these doctrines which are passed down from one generation to the next. If anyone decides to break free from these beliefs, they soon become the black sheep of the family or the odd bod, perhaps through deciding to think for themselves and thus have the chance to believe or not what they have been taught.

We came to this world to experience and explore everything, and even though we sometimes meddle in things which do not concern us, albeit with good intentions, it is because we believe that it is in the best interest of others. We have more than enough work with ourselves, so it is better to stay out of other people's lives unless they specifically ask for our help and advice. If I believe something to be positive for me, it automatically becomes positive for me, although someone else may not share my point of view. However, if I become truly convinced that the subject in question is negative, that energy becomes negative. If I have adored white chocolate all my life and suddenly someone persuades me that I am doing wrong in eating it, I begin to believe that anything that goes pear-shaped in my life is due to me eating white chocolate, and it starts to disagree with me. What has happened? My way of thinking has changed, I have started cocreating differently, and I have focused on what attracts my attention at that moment and labelled it as harmful to me. It is like producing poison. My subconscious emits the message that white chocolate is poisonous and my body requests a reaction from my immune system which sets off all the alarms. All the more reason to go ahead and enjoy whatever you fancy without having that monster behind you, telling you what you should or should not do or eat.

Allow me to tell you a story. During a phase of my life, I was a strict vegetarian. I wanted to explore the reactions that this lifestyle had on my body and to tell you the truth, at that time and for many years, I can assure you that I had never felt better. I became a long-distance runner, bursting with physical and vital energy in all aspects. I could run a marathon on just a quarter of a water melon for breakfast. Eventually, due to my work, trips and meals away from home, I had to vary my diet and incorporate some fish and chicken from time to time so as not to fall into the monotonous menu of pasta, omelette and boiled rice.

On one occasion, I was invited to an exquisite restaurant in Vigo, Spain where we were served a plate of Iberian Bellota ham as an aperitif. I decided to have a bit of fun and asked one of my colleagues to take a photo of me about to eat a piece of ham. My intention was not to eat the ham but to make the photo public on Facebook, with the following caption: "Caught, red-handed", to see how people reacted. I received hundreds of answers: "Suzanne, how disillusioned I am"; "Suzanne, you're eating a dead body", etc.

What is more, I had not even mentioned whether I had eaten that piece of ham or not. People assumed that I had. Although I must admit that originally, it was never my intention to eat a single piece of ham, I ate half of what was on the plate! I was thoroughly delighted, enjoying something which I had not done in twenty years, because I wanted to and at the same time, was breaking away from certain beliefs and taboos. It was a one-off experience, but I had to break free from that state of inflexibility and remember that we are here to try things out without clinging to dogmas or pre-established beliefs, not even those which are for our own good. Without feeling the slightest bit guilty, I thanked the pig whose meat had satisfied my taste buds and wished it all the best on its journey of evolution. Thus, the pig went on its way in peace, and my colleague and I too were at peace. If I had eaten the ham thinking that it was bad for me, it would have made me feel ill. Nevertheless, to aid my digestion, I chose fresh pineapple for dessert.

It was strange to see how my friends on Facebook acted among themselves. While some gave little importance to the issue, others were adamant that I had disappointed them. The vegans said that I had gone bananas and got myself in a pickle, as would be expected from vegetarians, but the incident gave rise to some excellent reflections and lessons learnt. It made a wonderful subject for debate, based on an experience one hundred per 'Zen' true!

The importance of being able to "cancel"

Now that we realise the existence of the power of our mind, our words and everything that we can imagine in a moment along with all the consequences, we need an immediate device to be able to eliminate anything that we have mentioned or imagined that we do not wish to become reality. As we understand the strength of our words, whenever we say something that we would rather not see manifested in our lives and we are aware of this at that moment, we can say to ourselves or out loud the word "cancel" and go on to rephrase the word or sentence. I may say, for example: "My life is a disaster". But when I ask myself if really want to live a disastrous life, the answer is "no". So, I simply say "Cancel" and then rectify: "My life is wonderful".

It makes no difference whether you believe it or not at the time. The word comes first, in the same way as the Bible describes Creation: "In the beginning was the Word". If we choose to transform our lives, deciding that we will live in a particular way, we are aligning ourselves with that particular lifestyle. If I say, for example: "I want to find love", I will live the experience of wanting to find love rather than actually living an experience of love. However, if I change my sentence to: "I experience love my whole life through", placing love at the top of my list, everything that appears listed below will be blessed with love. When this happens, EVERY SITUATION I EXPERIENCE IS THE TRUE EXPRESSION OF LOVE.

We must remember the existence of the Law of Polarity. In order to learn what exists on one side, we must know what the corresponding expression is on the other. To recognise what love is, we must recognise what that lack of love is like, and be prepared to embrace both experiences. Similarly, in order to accept a sunny day, we must be able to appreciate a day of rain and instead of grumbling about it, regard it as a blessing, because without it, there would be no place for the sun on our planet.

We must accept everything just as it is and overcome everything that Life offers us. If you laugh a lot, be prepared to cry a lot too, because EVERYTHING MUST BE IN PERFECT HARMONY. Observation is a key factor in the process of self-mastery. Through observation, listening and feeling we learn much more than when talking. If you want to know what you are really like, observe your reality and the people around you. There are many universal laws, and one of them is LIKE ATTRACTS LIKE; whether the outcome is something much better or something much worse, it enables you to realise the extent of your evolution without judgement. We must observe everything with modesty in order to be able to grow. A more evolved being is worthy of our admiration, and encourages us to improve some aspect of ourselves. We would like to be like that person.

There are different degrees of evolution. Some people find themselves at that stage of the process where you began; so do not look down on them in egoistic superiority but consider them with heart-felt humility. As if you were a speck of light. If you fall into the trap of feeling superior, you will cease to be an example and your vibrations will diminish. And as a consequence, your personal development will be affected.

If you find it difficult to be fully conscious while leading your life and you feel that you cannot control your mind, your impulses or your reactions or that you do not vibrate with the present moment, or that you have trouble sleeping and being happy, forgiving, forgetting and accepting others, do not despair: there is a solution called "RESET". My colleagues from the Zen course, who are capable of performing a reset, will help you eliminate those mental blocks and amassed burdens.

Let me explain what reset is: imagine a human being as a biological computer which is born with its own hard disk and main programme. The mind is the physical part where the software from this lifetime is stored, and contains phobias, apprehensions and beliefs. When a reset is carried out the operating system is treated, just as in the work of a computer technician, by means of energy points. A reset, with those energy points, manages to dispose of the erroneous software and place it in the recycle bin. Once the process, which takes about five minutes, has been completed the person experiences a feeling of inner peace as if he had shed a great weight. From then on, he can enjoy intense calmness and a reconfigured nervous system. His mental state is more harmonious and unbiased, at least at that moment, because sometimes it is necessary to reformat his mind.

That is why I like to say after a reset: "Your wish is my command. From this moment on, everything you think, say, imagine or feel will become reality. Make sure it`s good!"

It has always been like this but we are not aware of it. After a reset, I recommend you reflect on your life and connect your actions and reactions. Observe your words and the results, and associate your words and thoughts with any incidents. Sometimes, years may pass between the spoken word and the results or consequences. That is the case of a friend of mine who once told me: "I've always known that I'll marry a man called Charles". Years later she married a man by that very name. Was it in her programme or did she create the experience through her wishes? What difference does it make? Her wish came true, her words became actions.

Once the reset has been carried out, we can also co-create a new existence, providing that we understand that whatever we say or feel, and however we are or vibrate at this moment so shall be tomorrow, our future. It is essential to be conscious of what we think and feel, here and now. The vibrations I transmit today will determine what I experience tomorrow. How about you? What are you thinking and feeling and on what vibrational frequency? Are you vibrating with enthusiasm, unconditional love, happiness and the innocence of a child, knowing that all your wishes will come true and that you will want for nothing? Or are you perhaps thinking with a limited mind which will consequently limit your experience? To quote a good friend of mine: "We are masters of limitation".

Enough of exploring the limited mind; it is time to start and discover the unlimited mind. That is why I commented in my previous book, *The Collective Reset*: "If you want to consciously create, imagine yourself in the best situation, in perfect company and visualise this dream vividly in your mind, free of the limits of past experiences". You may like to say: "This is what I wish for or something MUCH BETTER". Our mind might not be able to imagine exactly what the Universe has got in store for us. Therefore, why limit the experience? Once this concept is established in our mind, it begins to expand and we not only want the best for ourselves but also rejoice in the success of others around us, free of envy, given that whatever we desire for others we also desire for ourselves.

If we surrender to our Self with this knowledge and we ask to be led along the most enriching path, we must accept all the consequences, knowing that everything that happens to us from then on is exactly what we need to grow towards a higher level of evolution. Even when we find ourselves subjected to a tragedy or conflict, we must understand that that situation is to our advantage, considering the fact that everything, including negative experiences, can help us in our personal development.

If we accept and embrace everything that happens to us, half the work is done. We must not resist nor refuse to accept that reality. It is better to allow what must be to be, with a calm mind and composure, through meditation and relaxation... basically, you must remain in the eye of the storm where all is still despite the world spinning out of control. That means being centred. Be your centre.

The more we progress in our evolution, the greater the feeling of tranquillity we experience and the faster we break free of our reactive mode. WHEN WE ARE IN REACTIVE MODE, OUR EGO IS SENSITIVE AND IS EASILY TRIGGERED OFF. It is inclined to protect itself by way of attack which is the best means of defence. It is very easy to lose control and say words which unrestrainedly rush out of our mouth and hurt others. However, we must remember that those words which are projected negatively always return sooner or later, like a boomerang, and hurt us too. We must be aware of this and accept all those experiences in our life which are necessary for our development.

It is interesting to observe people who have chosen to consciously pursue their evolution. THEY ARE EXTREMELY BRAVE INDIVIDUALS, PREPARED TO LEAVE THEIR COMFORT ZONE. They go all out and live life, with whatever risks this may involve. In the event of them subjecting themselves to danger – or alleged danger – and because they have nothing to live up to, others most certainly see them as having nothing to lose, but everything to gain. It is during those dangerous moments that they can make the most of all opportunities to continue progressing and review their barometer of spiritual growth.

A friend of mine often says: "It is not the circumstances that are important, but what you are in them".

CIRCUMSTANCES WILL OCCUR OVER AND OVER AGAIN THROUGHOUT YOUR LIFE UNTIL YOU LEARN THAT THEY IN THEMSELVES ARE NOT IMPORTANT. THE ONLY TRULY IMPORTANT ISSUE IS YOUR ATTITUDE TOWARDS WHAT YOU LIVE AND EXPERIENCE. THE ONLY TRULY DECISIVE ISSUE IS YOUR ATTITUDE TOWARDS EACH OF THESE CIRCUMSTANCES.

You have a right to stay in your comfort zone however long you wish, and enjoy that moment. Even that is perfect. But on your settee, with the TV remote control in your hand, do not point out, judge or criticise anyone who has decided to venture forth because one day, you may have to thank them for their action, whether you agree or disagree with their decision. Accept. And when you feel the time is right for you, stand up and leave the remote control behind. Take your place at the helm of your ship and dare to navigate amidst the storm towards a new life, leaving behind all attachments, and knowing that the time has come for you to explore the world, the unknown.

Signals

How do we know when the time is right?

First, you must want to find it, just like when you sit in front of your computer and type into the search engine whatever it is that interests you. Then you give the search engine time to find all the options. The key is very simple: first place your order, verbally or in writing, and then just forget about it.

*Inner curiosity is necessary in order to find what you are looking for.
Without action or intention, the answer will never arrive.*

There will be no signals to guide you and point you in the right direction. You must flow from the heart and become the observer of your own experience. At first, you will go through the initial phase of asking yourself if this or the other is happening by chance or if it is merely a coincidence. You may say to yourself: "What a coincidence! I keep seeing the number 22 wherever I look". And you are surprised to repeatedly see the number 22 everywhere: on a car number plate, as part of a telephone number, your seat on the plane... it might appear to be an amazing coincidence. And if you do not start asking yourself about what links you with this number rather than a different one, this information will be of no use to you whatsoever. This is where the game begins.

I can use the number 22 as a code, a type of signal. I declare: "When I see the number 22, I will ask myself what is happening at this moment, what I am thinking about, or if I feel something in particular, or even what I have just said, whereby the number 22 wants to attract my attention". The moment a signal appears, a repeated number or some detail that catches my attention time after time, I will interpret that signal as the confirmation of what I was thinking, feeling or saying. It will serve as a huge "yes, do it".

I can consciously ask my Self, whenever I need any kind of confirmation, to show me the number 22. A more definite confirmation could appear as 2222. As if by magic, the amusing game of life by signals begins. I happen to look at my watch and I see that the time is 22.22; a car goes past and I see that it's number plate ends in 22; I bump into someone and when they give me their phone number it contains the number 22 which tells me that I should call them without fail because they will convey some kind of connection or information to me.

All this can happen with any number. I chose the number 22 because as a child, when I was asked to choose a number between one and ten, I would always decide on four which in fact was the sum of 2 + 2. If I could choose a higher number, I would decide on 2222.

What is important is not the code or signal, but your reaction when it appears. IF IT IS IMPORTANT ENOUGH TO CATCH YOUR ATTENTION, USE IT. If there is a number that resonates with you, or any other sign that may be used as a signal, start playing with it. Use it. Pay attention to those moments when it appears. ALWAYS ASK YOUSELF WHY IT APPEARS AT THAT MOMENT. It will make you sigh, make you happy and give pleasure to your soul. And at one of those moments you may find yourself dining with twenty two people seated at the table. Or someone might give you a present which contains that number. What does it mean? Why now? You must ask yourself that. At times, the reason will not be very clear, but it might just be a practice-run.

The important thing is to be alert, conscious and awake so that when we are familiar with the exercise, we realise that this signal appears as confirmation of something important in our life.

It could even be a song that you hear over and over again, which gives you a feeling or reminds you of someone which suddenly transports you to a decisive moment in your life and you remember the happiness you felt at that time, and causes your soul to lift in the present. When this happens, you are reconnecting with your Self, making contact and giving rise to inspiration. Any action which moves your soul and rings true with you, making you feel the joy of living is a sign that you are in harmony with your Self. At times like these, your vibrational frequency rises and everything seems to be connected as if by magic.

Watch out carefully for all signals. BROADEN YOUR OUTLOOK TO A FULL SCREEN, JUST AS CHILDREN INNOCENTLY DO; THANKS TO THEIR WIDER VISION OF REALITY AND THEIR SHARPER SENSES, THEY CAPTURE ALL THE SIGNALS. They may even know intuitively what you are going to say. Somehow, they can read your mind and know how you are going to react. That is why it is easy for them to manipulate you. They are just exploring innocently with no bad intentions, how to catch your attention. We adults are usually less receptive because we are always chained to our mind and fail to see the signals as easily. We tend to reason too much instead of flowing with our intuition. That is why we usually dismiss the first feelings or instincts which are generally the most important, despite us considering them as not valid because our mind says: "Yes, but...".

WHEN YOU FEEL THE INCENTIVE TO ACT, THAT INSPIRATION DOES NOT ORIGINATE IN YOUR MIND, BUT IN YOUR HEART, OR YOUR HARD DISK, BECAUSE WHEN YOU ARE *IN SPIRIT,* THE ACTION DOES NOT FLOW FROM THE MIND BUT FROM THE VERY BEING. Only the mind will reject inspiration with a "yes, but...", "it can't be", "that's not true", or "it's not feasible", in an attempt to reason out what is happening. When we feel inspired, we know how to interpret the signs because at that moment the intervention of our mind gives way to the profound connection with our Self.

Observe. When you concentrate your attention on what you wish to achieve, your request is multiplied. For example, when a woman finds out that she is pregnant, she starts to see expectant mothers everywhere. When someone breaks their arm, they suddenly see lots of other people with their arm in plaster. However, if you do not pay attention to the signs, you will not notice anything and you will live in complete unawareness.

On one particular occasion I was sitting with my daughter who had a high temperature and to keep her amused we played a game. I suggested:

"Let's create butterflies. We'll just spend a while repeating the word 'butterfly'; we'll say it, sing it out loud, even shout non-stop the word 'butterfly'".

As it happened, that day I could not go to the therapy centre because my daughter was not well, so clients had to come to my home. What was amazing was that three of these people arrived with presents containing butterflies: a box with a butterfly engraved on the lid, a hairclip in the shape of a butterfly and a packet of butterfly stickers. With each of the presents we received, my daughter commented:

"Have you seen what we have created? It's true, it works... we have produced butterflies.

And with these surprise presents her fever disappeared. She began to enjoy the presents we had created. Ever since, these insects have followed us. The effect lasted longer than we imagined, and even now, wherever we go, we find butterflies.

Once, we saw one born in a butterfly conservatory and it was a truly incredible experience. In Fuerteventura (Canary Islands) we were taken into the dining room of the hotel, where the walls were covered with butterflies. It is a joy to see how they are always with us.

Not long ago, having recently arrived in Malaga (Spain), we were taken to visit another grand butterfly conservatory. It made me think about the life of a butterfly and metamorphosis. They are born and live the first stage of their life as a caterpillar. Then they turn into a chrysalis. After a while, they are born as a butterfly. What a vast transformation of a being in one lifetime. As one stage finishes, another completely different one begins, even more wonderful than the one before. The miracle of Life is intricately connected with constant change, that of transition.

At that moment, I realised that the transformation we undergo as human beings is that of knowing how to live as a caterpillar and be reborn as a butterfly, a new luminous being capable of flying and capturing the whisper of the air in its flight. Just when the caterpillar thinks that the end of the process is near, another one begins, immersed in stillness to give physical form to its magnificent free being, winged and colourful, whose beauty radiates so much inspiration.

When you pay attention to the signals, understanding how to interpret the messages they convey and you can set aside the notion of coincidence, life's magic begins to unfold, as nothing happens by chance. Everything is perfectly orchestrated. Depending on your level of consciousness, you will masterfully guide your own boat to where you want to go, instead of drifting downstream.

Magic moments

The first magic moment I was aware of was when I had just turned seventeen and was working as an au pair with a family in the south of Spain. To put me in the picture the lady of the household commented on things that had happened with the previous au pairs. She drew my attention to one English girl in particular who had spent the previous summer at her home looking after her three children. She told me that this girl had stolen a valuable ring which was the reason behind her dismissal.

That summer was especially difficult for me, being an experience of independence so far away from my family at home in Ireland and at the service of a well-to-do family in a foreign country. I was just a young inexperienced employee. I remember trying to do my best to please them, giving English classes, ironing, cleaning and helping the children, all of which I found far from easy. I was under the orders of a very authoritarian person. However, it was a wonderful opportunity for me to mature, to improve my knowledge of the Spanish language at such a youthful age and at the same time, to learn to appreciate what I had left back home.

A couple of days before I left for Ireland again, the lady of the house accused me of stealing her daughter's watch, which was a far cry from the truth. Naturally, I felt very angry. In a house full of tension, she made me empty my suitcase, but of course found nothing. I went to Madrid to visit an Irish girl-friend of mine who had also worked as an au pair in Spain. We sat on the steps leading up to the Post Office and exchanged our experiences from the summer. She had been in Soria and I had been in Andalusia. It was while we were talking there, under a blazing sun, that I noticed a very pregnant woman who was sitting on a step a bit further down from us with her young children, and I commented to my friend: "Look at that poor lady, with such a huge belly and those little kids, on a hot day like this; she must be having a really bad time with this heat".

At this comment, the lady turned round and asked me what the time was in perfect English. I wished I could have disappeared into thin air, realising that she must have heard everything we had said. Imagine my surprise when she enquired: "Have you been working with the Morales family this summer?"

"Yes. How do you know about that? I answered.

"Well, I worked as au pair with that family too four years ago and I recognised the names of the children you were talking about. When you said that they accused you of stealing a watch, I remembered my experience with them when they accused me of stealing a ring.

In surprise, I asked: "Are you Theresa?"

I could not believe my ears, that this lady was the au pair who had been in the same house where I had worked that summer. When I returned to Andalusia, to the Morales family's house, I explained what had happened and we managed to tie up loose ends and discovered that it was the daughter who was behind the false accusations in an attempt to get rid of any au pair because she did not want to have English classes.

That was the first time that I understood the meaning of perfect synchronisation. Can you imagine the situation?

It made me start to question lots of things and forced me to ask myself a lot of questions about that encounter. I needed inner peace and that lady provided it. Hearing her confirmation that the accusation was untrue was calming for me. Everything is fine, everything was fine. I could not have returned to Ireland feeling angry like I did. Everyone has their own reality and their own reason. The lady of the house was very upset to discover what her daughter had done.

I visited that household again, some ten years later. The children were ten years older and we could chat and recall the experience of those two and a half months of being together with joy and good humour, and even the little girl, by then twenty two years old, admitted to her dishonest method of getting rid of the au pairs. Everything worked out well in the end.

Another magic moment which happened recently was when my friends 'kidnapped' me to take me off to a health spa, seeing me in need of a rest and wanting to treat me to the experience. While we were in the changing room, still undressed, and enjoying feeling so relaxed after the spa session, another lady, also undressed, asked me while I was combing my hair near the shower:

"Are you Suzanne Powell?"

"This is a version of me", I answered.

"I can't believe it. I recognised you by your voice. Today is my birthday and my sister has treated me to a spa session. I am an avid fan of yours, I've attended your courses and I was just waiting for the right moment to make an appointment for a reset, seeing as I'm recovering from cancer.

I begged her to give me a few minutes to get dressed and I treated her to a reset in the changing room. She was truly grateful for this unexpected birthday present. It is beautiful synchronisation, seeing how the Universe grants you, albeit in a strange way, your wishes.

She requested it and she received it. And precisely on her birthday. She would never have imagined receiving a gift like that. I felt very happy seeing her so happy. When we left the spa, we were surprised to see how we had been fined for having gone over the time limit. But we arrived in time to cancel the penalty, by paying the compensatory amount.

Another memory I fondly cherish is that of an experience that happened some fifteen years ago when I was working as a lecturer in orthomolecular nutrition and medicine. One early Sunday morning, I had to leave home in the middle of a storm wearing an executive suit, high heeled shoes and carrying a briefcase. I needed a taxi but there was not one in sight at the time, so I stayed in the entrance hall, wondering what to do, as there was not a soul in sight. Somewhat desperate due to the time, I asked the Universe to please send me a taxi. Suddenly, out of the blue, a motorcyclist who was going in the wrong direction came up onto the pavement and stopped in front of me. He lifted the visor of his big black helmet and kindly asked me: "Do you need a taxi?"

I was so taken aback that it took me all my time to say yes. I can still remember what he looked like. He was tall and clad in a black leather suit. He continued in the wrong direction along the same road and turned off to the left. I thought that he was mad. Where had he come from and where was he going? Hardly a minute passed when a taxi appeared and stopped in front of me. The taxi driver opened his window and said to me: "This taxi is for you".

I thanked him and looked towards the end of the road where the motorcyclist was stationed with his visor up. He blew me a kiss with his hand, put his visor down and went off in the right direction. I just stood watching, wondering who he was. I wished for him to come back but my angel did not return. I got into the taxi and with a broad smile, the taxi driver said: "Good morning, Princess Atlanta, where are we going today?

We held a rather warm conversation as if we had known each other all our lives. I told him what had just happened as I could not believe it. But he just said: "Life is just like that for princesses".

I gave the conference with a great feeling of happiness about how amazing life can be, truly overwhelmed with the surprise and magic of that incident. In the evening, I called my Master, who was away on a trip, and I explained everything that had happened. He found it quite normal. He merely gave me a hint of all that I had yet to understand in terms of the multidimensional state of human beings. He said: "Suzanne, you asked for help because you needed a taxi. The help arrived and the taxi too at that moment. Can you now see that there is no need to worry about anything? You will always have whatever you need to continue your journey.

That experience gave me a lot to think about. I even began to wonder if those people had been real or if they were angels who had appeared spontaneously from another dimension. I was overwhelmed with unanswered questions about all that had happened.

Another incident that I experienced was to do with a journey I made with my Master from France to the United

States. I was in Barcelona and he, having just arrived at the French airport, received a message over the loudspeaker system to go to the nearest information point. Once he arrived, the receptionist told him: "There is a call from Suzanne Powell for you".

He was about to answer but discovered there was nobody on the other end of the line. He thought: "That's strange. Why would Suzanne phone me at the airport?"

When he arrived in the USA, exactly the same thing occurred. They called him over the loud speaker and the story repeated itself, with nobody on the other end of the line. He began to think that something had happened to me. When he arrived home in the United States, his phone began to ring. It was me calling, and once I had said hello, he asked; "How did you know that I have just this minute arrived home, and why did you call me at both airports?"

I said that I did not know what he was talking about and that I had not phoned him anywhere. It was just at that moment that it had occurred to me to phone to see if he had arrived safely. He commented:

"How curious – we love each other so much that whenever we think of each other, at that very instant, a call is made. That means that on both occasions we have both thought simultaneously about each other with unconditional love. Remember that for the future."

A month after the death of my maestro, I received a call from the United states from someone I knew who left a message on the answering machine. I have saved that message despite the years that have gone by. Halfway through the message, there is a break and the voice of my maestro can be heard with a very important message for me. Then the other person's voice is heard again. I shared that message with other Zen colleagues and friends of mine who confirmed that it was his voice. That proved to me that love exists beyond physical life and that my maestro continues to watch over me and my daughter.

Magical moments are inexplicable, almost incredible. If you truly considered the idea of something occurring on this level, there would be zero possibility of it happening. You would deem it practically impossible and would just say: "Keep on dreaming".

Magical moments simply occur if we stay relaxed, without thinking about anything. They tend to happen precisely during these moments of mental stillness. We receive a piece of information or a source of inspiration, or even the solution to a problem that has been worrying us for some time. It is just a matter of learning to get rid of the mental thought patterns and find our inner peace and quiet, with our nervous system in harmony and our reactive state at a standstill. In other words, remain centred, in every possible and imaginable circumstance.

> During these moments of tranquillity, we are able to access our hard disk, our I Am, our true Self, our essence, our God, depending on how you wish to call it.

Only during these moments of calm and absence of the mind can the data be transmitted from the Universal centre to our own. From then on, we can interpret that information through calm consciousness.

Other magic moments may occur in a state of wakeful-
ness, just when you are waking up from a dream or state of
sleep. The mental body is the non-physical body, or in other
words, that eternal body that travels in search of information throughout the universe and throughout all of our lives.
We could even state that its path is determined by our own
request or free will, and when it returns with the necessary
information, this 'software' is stored in the 'hard disk' – or
multidimensional super-memory of the mental body – until
our conscious mind requires it.

The hard disk or super-memory is located in the four-
th chakra, in the centre of the chest. It is that special place
where we experience that feeling or palpitation when we are
head over heels in love; it is the place we point to when we say
'me'. What are we referring to when we point to our chest?
We do not address a place in our head, but in our chest. We
are indicating our true Self, where we genuinely dwell.

THERE IS WHERE YOU WILL FIND YOUR MASTER, YOUR
TRUE MASTER; HENCE, YOU ARE THAT MASTER.

THERE, YOU ARE THE PUREST AND MOST EXALTED VER-
SION OF WHO YOU REALLY ARE.

To be your own master, you must be totally connected
with yourself, profoundly in touch with your soul. That is
where true freedom lies, leaving behind the unawareness of
not being and going forth to achieve infinite wisdom. As I see
things, and based on my own experience, TRUE WISDOM LIES
IN KNOWING WHAT YOU NEED TO KNOW THE MOMENT YOU
NEED THAT KNOWLEDGE. So, what is the point in worrying?
When you need to know something, it will come to you, not
before nor after, but at the precise moment. In that case, why

do we anticipate problems when they do not yet exist? You might even be creating them yourself, simply through paying attention to them, as this has the effect of transmitting to the Universe your request for problems to be generated. The rule is very simple: cross that bridge when you get to it, and not before.

When a potential problem arises in the future, just ignore it and consciously tell yourself: "Pay attention, I'm living in the present moment and I am not going to cross that bridge before time. When that problem presents itself, if it must present itself, I will have all the necessary tools to solve it". It is important to live in the present moment, immersed in harmony and consciousness, because the future does not exist yet and the past has already gone by. We can recalculate each moment, every instant, to adjust our life to what must be according to our programme.

Time

Blessed clock. We never have enough time to do everything we want to. We would like to do so many thing... but we just do not have the time.

In actual fact, we have all the time in the world. We can be masters of time. How many times have you noticed that time flies when you are having fun? On the other hand, those nights when you just cannot drop off to sleep, or when you are waiting impatiently for the first day of your holidays, time seems to last an eternity. In this illusory life, we think time is linear, when in fact, it is not like that. When we comprehend the multidimensional state of human beings, we realise that everything is based on frequency. We tend to think in linear terms, saying: "When I achieve this, I'll be able to do that or the other".

We direct our thoughts to attain a target and believe that it is impossible to achieve this unless we have undergone a series of events in time. We think that a certain amount of time is necessary to create what we want to experience or enjoy during our existence, instead of cocreating like children who believe in magic and the immediate manifestation of our wishes. The principle which declares: "Ask and it shall be given to you", is pure reality. They are always prepared to invent every kind of strategy to achieve their aims, at any cost. On the other hand, adults, who believe that some things are not possible, create their own limitations. They constantly repeat: "This can't be true". We are incapable of imagining how to attain something, without having a, b, c, d and the rest of the alphabet of circumstances which we believe are essential in order to achieve it. We may believe in shortcuts – and create them – instead of going through primary school, secondary school, A- levels and university to gain our degree in mastery.

The rule is: "Make it easy, be natural,
and do not complicate things".

I surrender to my Soul, thus simplifying my journey so that my desire to achieve mastery is manifest and all my dreams come true for my own good and for the good of others also. This allows me to enjoy my wishes and needs, be relaxed and take pleasure in every moment of my journey, observing how the shortest path reveals itself before my very eyes and inspires in me complete and utter trust in the fact that it is perfect and precisely what I need at this moment. There must be no resistance, no negation, no complaints, but total and full acceptation.

The principle of minimum effort is the swiftest path. Nothing requires effort, unless your limited mind is programmed to believe that you must fight to achieve what you need.

This is true. Actually, you do not need anything unless your mind believes that it requires a series of trials or circumstances to achieve its aims. However, it is quite the opposite: it is rather a case of relieving the load instead of accumulating even more in our rucksack. It is a matter of getting rid and practising total detachment. The less we pack into our rucksack, the lighter it will be and the easier for us to continue along our path of life.

Credits and deficits

To be masters of time, we must understand how the Law of Cause and Effect works, the Law of Equilibrium. If you are in a hurry to attain abundance, happiness and love, you only have to eliminate everything which is preventing you from achieving harmony. If you desire love, give love. The more you give, the more you will amass for yourself. If you live in conditions of scarcity, share the little you have and observe how it comes back to you. If you are depressed, find someone you can shower with smiles, as there is always someone worse off than yourself. On receiving a smile, just feel the happiness that you never dreamed possible and suddenly, you find a way of emerging from that hole which keeps you slumped in depression.

To be masters of time, it is essential to comprehend how everything in the Universe is cyclical. There are cycles of a year, or twelve years, monthly cycles and menstrual cycles, sun and moon, cosmic... Everything comes back to you, according to the Law of Action and Reaction: whatever you give always returns to you. When you realise that this is always true, you begin to take more care about what you give, making sure that all your actions, words, feelings and intentions spring forth from unconditional love. The more acts of unconditional love, deeds of benevolence and expressions of dedication you carry out, the more credits you amass in what I call 'the Bank of Divine Providence'.

The shorter the time lapse between the wish being made and its appearance, the more credits collected in your favour. And when the results are instantaneous, in other words, you ask and immediately receive, this means that you have become an excellent master of time because you know that time no longer exists and that you do not need to do anything to attain whatever you require. You have learnt to live in abundance and wisdom because you are in harmony with the Universe and with yourself. Do you fancy a chocolate ice-cream? Fine, the Universe takes note and at that very moment someone passes by and offers you a chocolate ice-cream. It does not matter why or how it has happened; as if by magic, your wish has simply come true. Magic takes place and true mastery has been reached when the Universe offers you a freezer full of ice-creams for you to choose from and share with all your friends.

Time does not exist. Everything is ephemeral; so, there is always time to do what you really want to. You only have to specify your priorities and be ever ready to modify them if necessary. Your preferences can be changed along the way depending on the circumstances. Nothing is important, unless you decide to make it so.

Sometimes, parents make an appointment to see me with their adolescent sons and daughters and ask me to carry out a reset so that they will be better organised with their studies, leisure time, friends, and in short their whole lives, to the liking of their parents. I just listen to those youngsters, and try and put myself in their place in order to understand their concern, dissatisfaction, frustration and personal limitation because they do not know how to attain the expectations created by their predecessors.

In front of their parents, I discuss how they must live their own lives, follow their own path and discover their gift or talent in order to be happy. I point out that the educational system is outdated, full of old fashioned standards and obsolete prototypes, and therefore, is not compatible with them. It is the new generations who must change the system with their energy, their non-conformism with old-fashioned institutions and their repudiation of outdated rules.

I talk to them of the importance of respect towards their parents and teachers, but also of the need to pursue their dreams despite the expectations of others. Every child is gifted, having a special talent, something that he or she can do better than anybody else in the world. But children need the necessary encouragement to be at peace and feel truly inspired by that which inevitably can make them happy. If we give them this support, they will find themselves on the correct frequency and will enjoy complete and utter freedom to creatively express their full potential, fearless of criticism, prejudice or mockery.

Not long ago, I had an appointment with a fifteen year old boy who, according to his mother, was totally idle because he did not want to study. He was bored at school; he saw it as "a drag", as many other children do. They may be interested in a couple of classes, but why do they have to attain good grades in all subjects? Because according to the system, which says that if they do not pass their exams, they will be nobodies, unable to earn their living. That is why parents make the mistake of putting pressure on their children, because they want them to be 'someone' in life. To follow this pattern is to deny the existence of a new Mozart, Einstein, Beatles, Borges or Velazquez in the present day.

When I asked this boy what he was good at, what he loved doing, some talent that he had that nobody else had, he looked at me completely bewildered, so while I gave him a nudge, I asked him in his own jargon: "Hey, mate. What gives you a buzz?"

His mother interrupted us, saying: "He's a great magician".

With a look, I asked her to remain silent and let her son speak for himself, so that I could tune into to the boy talking about performing magic tricks. I told him of friends of mine who were magicians, I showed him some photos of special effects that sometimes occur during the courses I give, and told him, how in a way, I was a magician, doing magic with people who asked for my help. His eyes opened wider and wider in surprise.

I went on to assure him: "Don't worry about school. To keep your parents happy, pass your exams but don't waste your time doing what makes you unhappy or down in the dumps. Just do what is necessary and spend the rest of the time doing what you are best at so that you may become a true master of what you have come to do in this lifetime.

We dedicate so much time doing useless things! Do we ever consider just how much time we waste? Or just how little time we afford to the game of life, to relationships, to whatever inspires us, to experiencing a wide range of feelings and exploring all the changes which occur in our life? Instead, we shut ourselves away in a dark room with artificial lighting and do any such other unfulfilling deed.

Whoever achieves excellent marks will be brilliant for a profession and everything will flow naturally with ease. Anyone who is *fighting* to attain good results will *fight* for the rest of his life to survive. Simply because he believes that to be 'someone' he has to put in a lot of effort. How many dissatisfied and frustrated professionals are there in the world today? Probably they would like to have a different job even though this implied earning less money. How many people live off what they truly love?

This brings us to an important question: What are we teaching our children? What kind of education are we giving them? They do not belong to us. They are just beings on loan to us, masters who come to help us in our own evolution. They teach us how to be parents, even though they arrive with no instruction leaflet. They give us the opportunity to experience unconditional love, patience, tolerance and acceptation. We love them just as they are, or at least we should do. We cannot expect them to be as we were because times have changed. We must learn to be as innocent as children instead of showing them how to be adults. It is the father's or mother's ego that imposes its standards and beliefs: "You must do this or that, because I say so!" We have a lesson pending, that of learning humility and respect towards our children, a lesson of mastery for the parents.

> The best way to attain mastery is to retrace your
> steps in order to redeem your inner child.

How can we reencounter our inner child? By giving ourselves permission to be like a child, with the same innocence and honesty. By expressing our feelings freely. By discussing openly our worries, frustrations, discontentment, desires and yearnings. By humbly expecting nothing in return, neither reward nor recognition. By being fearless of rejection and mockery. If we were all like children, there would be Paradise on Earth.

Food for thought: Visualise the scene of playtime at a children's primary school. The more little ones, the better; there is less mind activity, less programming and more naturalness and spontaneity. In the playground there are various games set up in different areas. We can see how a large group of children come out of the classroom and each child freely stands at the game which appeals to him the most. The groups are formed according to the preferences of each child.

The children will make the most of the time to fully enjoy the game. They will not abandon a game to go running off and try them all but will stay at the current one while they are making the most of it. When they are tired, they will look for some other amusement, another group, but without getting caught up in the mental process of which would be the best. The child acts on vibrations and without fear, in an instinctive way, just as animals do. In the same way at home, if someone who is bad tempered, depressed or drunk pays a visit to the household, the child will shy away, feeling the need to seek refuge in his mother's skirt. On the other hand, when someone who is loving, joyful and jubilant arrives, the child will be attracted to him if the feeling is genuine and the vibration is positively real.

Back at the playground, once playtime is over, the children happily go back to their class, having enjoyed being present during that spell of fun.

Now let us imagine sending the adults to the playground and telling them: "You have an hour to do what you want". What is the first thing the adults do? LOOK AT THEIR WATCH. Time is the most important thing for the adults while for the children, only the present moment exists. After that, the adults try out all the different kinds of amusement within their reach, instead of enjoying just one, because time is ticking by.

What concerns them the most? What will they pay attention to? The adult will always select a game or group via a filtering system. He does not possess a natural instinct to explore through pure pleasure, with all the consequences, but will be manipulated by the code of fear and caution that is integrated in him. He will mentally analyse, little by little, where he fits in the best. He will look for the game and the group which are best suited to his tastes, preferences, and fears without allowing himself to be carried along spontaneously. Inevitably, he will be swept off by preconceptions and will be afraid that the rest of the group will not accept him.

Some may want to stand out, others will want to pass unnoticed, and some will want time to go by quickly, while others want playtime to last longer. They will all be busy mentally analysing rather than heartily enjoying the present moment, in the most appropriate, fitting place. Why not be like children and take pleasure without needing to know everything, try everything and investigate everything? Which playground is more to your liking? Which playground would you choose in order to feel freer, more yourself? How many things do we do nowadays for the pure pleasure of it?

WE ARE ALL IN SEARCH OF HARMONY, the freedom to pursue our journey in Life, experiencing and feeling harmonious love which is the key to happiness. But we must respect everyone's pace, knowing that happiness is only a sign that we are on the right track. For this reason, we should judge no-one, because EVERYONE LIVES LIFE AT THE IDEAL PACE FOR THEIR OWN LEARNING, EXPERIENCE AND EVOLUTION. Therefore, we need to simplify things and relax; flowing freely without creating hopes or demands of perfection. We should adopt the attitude: "I have enough on with myself. Why spend time trying to change others, just so that I feel more at ease?"

Remember that it is difficult to grow in the comfort zone. As I pointed out in my previous book, *The Collective Reset*, it is the person who touches a sensitive spot, who puts you on edge, makes you lose your temper or drives you up the wall, who is your true master because he is proving to you that you have not yet attained self-mastery. Thank them for that and accept gracefully that you still have a lot to learn.

Where do we usually find these spiritual guides? Without a doubt, they are within our own family because we have to 'put up with them' for life, with no way out. We have the karmic opportunity to overcome our weaknesses while living alongside our children, brothers and sisters and parents because somehow they are there to help us find our own karmic balance. It is a valuable opportunity to learn.

When we leave the family home, we naturally tend to look for a partner. Once again we are looking for balance, harmony, peace and happiness. And we will only attract towards us that mirror which will reflect what is inside us at the time, with the vibration that we are transmitting or sending out in those circumstances. If you do not like what appears in the world you live in or the people you come into contact with and with whom you spend a great deal of your time, reflect on that and look inside you. Consider: "What must I change inside me in order to change what happens outside?"

For example, if I look at myself in the mirror and I see that my hair is a mess, it is useless combing my image in the mirror. To change this reflection, I must comb my own hair. This comparison is perfect to help us understand how our inner world is reflected in the outer one.

When this kind of teacher appears in our life as our partner, we should internally thank them for giving us the opportunity to be a renewed, more updated version of ourselves. Everybody who crosses our path is an angel, often strangely disguised, who affords us the opportunity to grow, even though it might not seem so at the time. We should always give heartfelt thanks for their presence, and never complain.

It is of no use to regret constantly what we have been through in the past or look for culprits, because by living in the past we pick up that frequency and bring it to the present, thus cocreating our future. As a result, the future will just be a continuation of what we have lived in the past. So, what can we learn from this? The past is the past; therefore, the best way is to forgive, forget and accept. And it goes without saying, we must always say 'thank you'.

Today I am a new version of who I was yesterday and tomorrow I will be a new version of who I am today. By universal law, or by actual life cycles, sometimes people reappear from the past; people with whom we have endured friction, conflicts or dislikes and who have given us the opportunity to settle old scores and find harmony and balance through forgiveness, oblivion and acceptance, but now in a revised version. For this reason, we should never judge anyone for their deeds, words or feelings from the past; we should be prepared to receive that person with the freshness and joy of the new version that is in front of us. Inevitably, we all change.

What kind of partner would you choose for your future development? Someone who is akin to the new consciousness, knowing that this choice will enable you both to progress together? You only need to focus on what you feel in the presence of that person. Your assessment must be based on how you feel when you are with them, and not on how they make you feel. It is no good making them responsible for how they make you feel, in terms of happiness. This way, instead of using expressions like: "You make me happy", we can say: "I feel so happy when I am with you". It is better to avoid prospects such as: "While you are like this and you behave this way, I will love you, but if you change, we're through". When we feel complete, we can observe how we feel in the presence of others. Obviously, we will have our preferences, depending on the degree of our evolution and the level of our awareness. Like attracts alike.

Our progress and level of evolution towards mastering this kind of love is put to the test when we say: "I am happy with you and also without you. I am happy when you are happy. I give you complete freedom to be who you are and how you are. And if you are ever happier with someone else rather than with me, I give you the freedom to continue your path of life by their side. I will be happy for you and also for the other person". This kind of love is a mature love. We must not try and put obstacles in the way of our partner's freedom, giving rise to egoism and possession. Love is lived in the present moment. There may simply come a time when you do not fancy sharing your life with someone who does not offer the characteristics which help you to grow and develop. It is a wonderful experience to share this new version of yourself with another being who feels the same way as you do. This is a harmonious relationship. One based on freedom and approbation. You will love this person with all their virtues and imperfections.

If at any time, we feel that the flame of love wanes, or we get caught up in routine and boredom, we must revive the romance, revitalise it, bestow it with freshness, inspire it with new rhythms and passions, and take a trip together or take a break. This means a short digression in time: "Darling, I'm going to spend a month or two to reflect on how I really feel. I'm asking you for this time for the benefit of both of us". But during this time, it would be more sensible to take care and avoid the temptation of experiences with other people. Just enjoy the time being without your partner.

With the passing of time, even our feelings change. The passion and novelty of the beginning are transformed into a mature love, more established and integrated, without being classed as boring. It is just a case of keeping the spark alive, constantly rekindling the relationship, incorporating new experiences, exploring unknown places, sharing with people from other surroundings. Perhaps a change of house, job or car would do the trick. Broaden your horizons.

Sometimes, according to the cycles of life, one partner of the relationship may be on a high, flowing along in a state of happiness, while the other is at a low ebb in spirits. Through unconditional love, the one who feels better will help the one who is downcast. Nobody stays permanently on a high and nobody stays eternally on a low. Everything changes, everything is transitory.

What many couples do not understand is that when one partner finds themselves immersed in a moment of depression or confusion, it is not the time for the other one to rush off in search of another partner, but the moment to support them. Perhaps you feel out of sorts today, but tomorrow I may feel the same. Everything is cyclical and we must be aware of the changes, always on the crest of the wave to see the complete perspective, everything that is happening, with detachment and mutual support. It is merely a case of being patient, since time heals everything and puts everything in its place.

These moments of hardship or conflict are moments for stopping, meditating and retiring to that state of calmness where we realise that the storm is not eternal and that nothing lasts for ever. It is during these moments that we grow because the comfort zone no longer exists. The wisest thing to do is observe how we react under the circumstances, how we overcome the force of habit.

It is delightful to hear elderly couples relate their love stories, those adventures of survival which enabled them to stay together for so many years, those tales of how they overcame the great trials love and see their countenances wrinkled by their constant smile in the face of life and its suffering. It is lovely to watch how they hold on to one another as they walk along the street. And to see how they still give that tender kiss, loving touch and knowing wink as they remember the good old days. These valuable experiences inspire me with humble affection and great faith and optimism.

In whatever the relationship, to attain mastery, we must be perfectly honest with ourselves. There must be transparent, open communication, but just saying what is necessary as words, once projected, cannot be retrieved. Creation has begun. As they say in the East: "TURN YOUR TONGUE SEVEN TIMES BEFORE SPEAKING".

If there is a moment of uncertainty and doubt, before jumping to conclusions and thinking something that could be wrong, just ask yourself: "What am I feeling right now, and why?" Rather than prejudge, we must remember that the person in front of us is a mirror. Perhaps his reality has nothing to do with us. Therefore, if you are angry, sad or confused or if you harbour negative thoughts, ask yourself why you feel that way. Better still, turn your tongue seven times and go for a walk and try and find out why you are projecting these feelings.

No-one is to blame for anything that is happening in your life. Put your hand on your heart and say to yourself:

"Mea culpa". First and foremost, accept yourself and forgive yourself. You are learning to be *human* so you do not need to be perfect nor demand perfection from anyone. WE ARE SPIRITUAL BEINGS LEARNING TO BE HUMANS. In any case, it is all a charmingly spectacular stage production where we are all discovering each other in the playground of Life. All together, we contribute variety and originality, amusement and sharing; each of us always unique and unrepeatable. At times, we may be a little confused because we do not understand the play script, but we are always trying to open up to self-mastery in order to follow its coordinates.

Follow your heart, not reason

Give your mind time off. Stop thinking so much. Opt to be happy doing what you feel you must do. Be yourself, with all the consequences this implicates. Open your heart and feel. The universe always gives you what is for your own good when you surrender to your Self, and not necessarily what you want. When your heart is open, you wish for what is in your best interest, and therefore there is total harmony between what you ask for and what you receive. Points are accrued in our credit account, but only when we allow ourselves to be led by our heart, by our Self, can we trade in this credit in accordance with the whole universe. So, you may grant yourself all your well-earned whims, provided you are in dancing in tune with the universe.

Grant yourself every whim

It is our right from birth to be happy. This happens when we surrender to our Self, to our purpose, our mission as humans. Give yourself permission to enjoy what takes your fancy and just as the universe decrees: "Ask and you will receive", so it shall always be. Sooner or later, your wish will come true. Accept everything you receive in life because the Law of Correspondence always sees to it that what is awarded to you is precisely what is appropriate for you at each moment.

Do not reject those whims – by thinking that you do not deserve them, for example – because this would implicate the refusal of abundance. You can share everything that reaches you with people who know how to value it and treat it with care. We often receive presents that we consider to be of little value, but perhaps they arrive with good intentions, or represent a significant effort made by the person who has offered us the gift. For this reason, every present is worthy of respect and gratitude.

My daughter, before opening any present that she receives, holds it against her chest, closes her eyes, smiles and without knowing what is inside, on instinct says: "This brings so much love with it!"

Children are always happy when their wishes are fulfilled. They feel lucky, they smile, and they jump up and down with joy and when they learn abundance, they love to share everything they receive, instead of selfishly keeping it to themselves, as impoverished people would do, regardless of what they have. Saving for tomorrow, *just in case*.

If we behave like this, saving for tomorrow, we are creating scarcity for the future. If you are lacking something it is because you have created that vibration and the universe has simply expanded it. The universe always creates abundance, always expanding whatever vibrations you project. It will even give you an abundance of scarcity!

How can we change this? We must first start with our thoughts and words, both spoken and written, and then work on creating abundance, giving what we want to receive. If you have little, dare to give it away and discover that you can be a MASTER OF ABUNDANCE. Just observe how when you give without expecting anything in return, everything comes back to you with increase. This is the Law of Abundance, the only secret of prosperity. Everything appears as if by magic.

Abundance means having what you need when you need it

Having abundance is having enough when you need it for yourself and your family. Every day, I ask myself if I have all that I need in order to do all that I need to do. And the answer is always: "Yes!" Why worry about tomorrow? When *tomorrow* arrives, in fact it will just be another *today*.

Let us take for example a pending debt, which is an important sum of money, as is the case with a lot of people nowadays, with the added risk of losing everything, even our house and belongings. The greatest lesson that we can learn from this situation is identifying exactly what we have to change to eliminate that mental burden and allow sufficient money to reach us in order to pay off the outstanding debt. If you are thinking of a debt, you are creating the vibration of *lack of abundance*. Therefore, you must think differently, think that your life is plentiful, and that you always have enough for whatever you need to do today, at present, in the now. Choose to be abundant with your time, your love, rejoicing in not only your abundance and wealth but in other people's stroke of good luck.

Rejoicing in the abundance or good luck of others, attracts towards you a new vibration that will be projected in your own life too.

Instead of thinking negatively, think positive thoughts, free of envy and mistrust. The more you actively hope for something, the more you distance and postpone it. It is like when a woman wants to become pregnant. She becomes anxious and her hoping prevents her dream from coming true. On the other hand, if she is happy for the fertility of her friends, she will attract the same for herself. So, if you have any outstanding debts and can free your mind of the idea that only money can settle a debt, you can get rid of this mental block and gain credits for your acts of love and devotion or through charity. In this way, some day and somehow, you will cause just the right amount of money to fall into your hands, whether it is from an inheritance, or a gift or an unexpected sale, which will help you to pay off your debt.

A friend of mine was awarded a plot of land as an unexpected inheritance on the death of a relative. He sold it and was able to clear his debts with his friends and family.

There is no need to dramatise the situation. We must not empower it either. At times, we see people overcome with troubles and misfortunes. It is advisable not to enter into the spiral of sympathising with the person affected, but rather try and play down the situation and try and help them understand that they must accept the circumstances, while changing their list of priorities for other more favourable ones. If they spend all day complaining about their hardship, the universe will simply expand that vibration, and as a result, they will attract experiences which give them all the more reason for complaint.

When someone tries to attract you into their spiral of sorrow and drama, you must try and defuse the situation. Make them laugh at themselves. Relieve their emotional baggage, no matter how miserable they appear and bring relief to the atmosphere too. Even the worst situations can become a circus if you dare play the game of being the best clown.

Allow me to tell you a story. We were on a trip with a group of Zen colleagues doing humanitarian work in Vietnam, which is something that you cannot do openly in a communist country like that. We had to bluff our way through to be able to help in leper colonies, orphanages, hospitals or disaster areas, among other places. On one of our trips, we were eating quietly at a school for poor children, where voluntary workers served the food. To our surprise, a police van pulled up at the door and the police came into the school declaring they had come to arrest us. The scare was enough to give us severe indigestion. I looked at my colleagues and gave them a sign to let me deal with the situation. The police wanted us to accompany them to the police station. I said:

"Look, we have a wonderful meal here and we are hungry. If you don't mind letting us stay to eat, we will not appear rude to our hosts. If you fancy joining us, you are welcome to eat with us".

The policeman I had spoken to looked at me disbelievingly and amazed. He could not credit what he was hearing. To my surprise, he agreed to letting us eat and said that they would be back to arrest us an hour later. It seemed illogical, considering the laws of a communist country. But they left. We sat down to eat and my friends could barely swallow. I said: "Look, we're in a situation that we must get out of. You are Spanish and French and I am Irish. Let me do the talking with the police. As I speak English, I will give the only possible version. It is compulsive for us to lie because in a communist country we cannot say that we are working for charity. So, nobody else is to admit to speaking English.

They were all very relieved by this decision, and an hour later, the police came back for us. I decided to meditate for a while to be completely at peace, to ask for help, to be clear-headed and to make the most of this great opportunity to grow. We were taken to the police station and I was separated from the rest of the group. The receptionist of a local hotel was with me to translate. Little did I know then that he would be my best ally.

When the interrogation began with the chief officer in uniform who wore a very severe expression on his face with a very military-like attitude, I realised just what I was getting myself into and remembered that we were in a communist country. I thought to myself: "I either make the most of the experience or I risk my life and that of my colleagues, seeing as they don't understand the word *freedom* here". I decided to play the role of an innocent, playful dumb blond. The questions began via the interpreter:

"What is your name?"

"My name is Suzanne Powell. And you sir, what is your name?" I answered.

The interpreter gave me a poker-faced look, but did his job. The next question was:

"How old are you?"

I answered him and returned the question. The interpreter looked at me, puzzled. From then on, whatever the chief police officer asked me, I also asked him. He went on to ask:

"Where did you spend last night?" I told him that the names of that country were very strange and I began to invent names with a Vietnamese accent, saying that I could not remember whether it was this place or the other.

The officer and the interpreter started to talk among themselves, somewhat frustrated, until the officer raised his arms in the air, hit the table and left. When I was alone with the interpreter, we started to talk and he asked me personal questions about my life, just to be polite and break the ice. He wanted to know what my religion was and when I said I was Catholic he warned me: "Whatever you say, don't say that because I am too and here it doesn't go down well". I took note.

Then a different officer came back into the room and proceeded to ask me the same questions as before. I continued to play the same role and repeated all the questions. The interpreter started to caution me, touching my foot slightly with his under the table, participating in my favour in the interrogation, which made me feel less alone. The new officer also became annoyed, stood up and left. The interpreter went after him and I was left alone. Despite the fact that I was putting on the act of being an innocent cutie-pie, I was scared stiff deep down and I could feel my back clammy with sweat.

The interpreter arrived with a third officer, who I noticed had several moles on his face from which sprouted long hairs; I found this amusing. I started to giggle and he asked me what I was laughing at. I told him that I was hungry and that my stomach was rumbling.

"Isn't there anything to eat or drink here? I'm hungry and thirsty", I told him.

He immediately got up and brought me some sweets and a glass of water. I remember asking him who the statue was. I continued with my act of the dumb blond since I knew full well who the statue was standing of: it was the political leader of Vietnam.

We continued with the same process of questions and answers. The interpreter warned me that this officer spoke English, although he pretended not to and that is where my game of pure and simple fun began, in the authentic Powell style. I started to let slip trivialities and puns until I caught him laughing even before the translation had been heard. At that, I pointed to him cheekily, and said: "You understood me before, didn't you?"

Question that he asked me, question that I asked him. And when he told me his age; I teased, saying: "I would never have thought that. You don't appear to be that old".

At that, he became very pleased with himself. In the end he walked out with a more carefree, unconcerned look than the previous two officers.

Alone with the interpreter once more he told me that I was completely insane. He said that no one dared to speak with the police like that, although with me they did not seem to mind. He warned me to be very careful. I told him not to worry and that I knew what I was doing.

As they took their time coming back, the translator went to see what was happening. He left me alone for quite a while, during which I could hear voices at the end of the corridor. Later, the interpreter returned alone and very worried, he explained that a Vietnamese lady among the volunteers, who had served the food, had also been detained. She had also been asked the same questions about our stay, our trips, the dates and what we were doing in Vietnam. However, her version did not correspond with mine, as we were both answering with lies; I was trying to prove that our trip was touristic and she was trying to cover up for us with her answers.

At that moment, I realised I just needed to relax because there had to be a solution somehow. All that I had learnt in my Zen training flashed through my mind. Then another officer who appeared to be the boss arrived and asked me the same questions all over again. He asked hundreds of questions – as I did to him – and he left just as confused as the rest.

He asked the interpreter to accompany him, and after a while, the interpreter returned with an announcement:

"Suzanne, this is a delicate situation that must be resolved. We know you are lying. The voluntary Vietnamese lady has been detained and your stories do not tie up. They are prepared to release you but cannot do so if your stories do not coincide. They have suggested that I tell you that when the next officer comes in, just answer yes to everything and you will be allowed to go. They like you because you are funny, friendly and daring and even though they know you are lying, they are going to free you.

When the next officer entered, I did not stop playing with all the questions, sometimes delaying the 'yes' and drawing out the pauses before answering, while others answering 'yes' even before the question had been asked. I could see that the officer was finding it very difficult to keep from smiling. His smile tugged at the corner of his mouth. Even his moustache twitched under the effort of holding back his smile.

I stayed a while with the interpreter when the officer left and after a time, I was taken to join my colleagues who were exhausted and worried. I appeared with an ear-to-ear grin and several kilos less in weight due to the tension and nerves. Eventually we were told to leave.

Outside the building, we met all the officers who had interrogated us, now dressed as civilians. Out of uniform, they looked like teenagers. They greeted me with smiles and hugs and the one who spoke English said:

"Well done. We have had a lot of fun with you, but take care not to do it again because anywhere else, you could have been wiped out without a trace.

When we got back into the police wagon, we took the opportunity to take a photo as a souvenir of that sombre place. When we got back to our quarters, it was suppertime. I remember how I sat on the settee and broke down crying, just to release the tension and a sigh of relief for having 'passed the test'. The game had turned out well. We hugged each other in celebration of our freedom and accepted everything cordially as a great experience.

What was the key to the whole episode? In fact, I had dared to be myself, without dramatising an experience which under normal conditions would have been a conflict or extreme situation. But by playing down the importance of the circumstances and applying a good dose of humour, I felt I had nothing to lose. I had to forget the rules, break free from mental concepts and play with the heart of those men in an original, unthinkable way that might give them motive for conversation at a later date: "Do you remember the Irish girl who dared to tease us?" To me, they were just human beings dressed in uniform acting out the role which corresponded to the code of authority and power. When they changed out of their uniforms and dressed as civilians, I understood how they were nothing more than typically normal playful lads. They were powerless because I had won the battle using the arms of an Irish woman: love and humour. I stripped them all.

The lesson was to CONVERT A MELODRAMA INTO A GAME. NOTHING HAS GREATER IMPORTANCE THAN THE IMPORTANCE YOU GIVE IT. It is imperative not to enter into that spiral of melodrama which absorbs and destroys. This experience was a wonderful opportunity to grow personally and to learn to behave differently in an unknown situation, out of the comfort zone. On another level, it may be that I chose to live this experience in order to climb a rung on the ladder more quickly, in terms of personal development.

On this path of mastery, we choose a field of learning and in this domain we have to use all the possible lessons to learn from each and every one. Once we learn the lesson on one level, we go on to the next.

We leave behind many admirers, disciples and companions who have interacted with us so that we can pass into a new zone where everyone knows more than we do. We once more become disciples of life. But we are still in sight of and in touch with our admirers from the previous link. Between one level and the next there is a GREY ZONE where it is difficult to distinguish clearly the correct path because there is a fork in the road with two possible directions. One way is the appropriate direction, the other is less suitable. In this dense zone of thick fog, from which we cannot see where the two roads lead to, there is a great deal of uncertainty because we do not know which of the two paths to choose. It is here that we must be totally modest and recognise our vulnerability and ignorance and accept that we do not know all the answers.

Our followers or disciples consider us as their guide and ask our advice to help them ascend a level. But at this stage, there is still a lot to learn. Everything is new. We must dare to make a decision with all the resulting consequences and to experience, always aware that we could be totally mistaken. If we take no risks, we learn nothing. And even though we take the plunge, careful with every step, or are absolutely convinced that we have chosen correctly, we must remain modest. Because UNTIL WE LEAVE THE GREY ZONE, WE WILL NOT KNOW IF WE HAVE MADE THE RIGHT DECISION OR NOT. ONLY THROUGH MODESTY AND ACCEPTANCE CAN WE ATTAIN

A HIGHER LEVEL. On the contrary, we must remain in that zone until we have learnt our lesson, albeit by encountering the same pitfalls over and over again. If we make a mistake, we simply admit to it.

When you find yourself in the grey zone, ahead of you are the people who have already emerged from it and these are the ones who will become your new guides and advisers, to be listened to with modesty as you are now the disciple and not the master. We could liken them to those advisors who, depending on your A level results, assess you and advise you on university degrees that you might choose from to pursue professional success.

They have a broader view and prospect than you have, because it is a completely new domain for you. You might fulfil the requirements but you will not know how to choose the best place to study. If you go forth blindly you run the risk of making a mistake. The same thing happens on all levels of evolution. We can consider it like a pyramid, with its different tiers until we reach the peak of absolute mastery.

There will always be beings who know more or less than you. They are neither superior nor inferior in any way, shape or form, but are simply beings that have experienced and advanced a little bit more or less than you. SELF MASTERY ALWAYS ARISES FROM MODESTY. We can say that there is no worse an ego than spiritual ego. When you fall to its prey, sooner or later you make a fool of yourself, because you always end up revealing your true self. Of course, there is always the temptation to boast about your spiritual progress. But generally, those who brag the most are the ones who know the least, while someone who remains quietly smiling probably is the most enlightened in the subject. The master must know how to adapt, through silence and modesty, to the level of consciousness of those around him. He must not give unwarranted information or advice which is irrelevant. His method of conveying such advice is by being an example and guiding his disciples towards the experience of situations to be learnt from. The true master invites his disciples to reflect and delve into the inner master within each and every one of us, with no recrimination, prejudice or bad feeling, of being different or inferior for not having been able to distinguish or see clearly during these moments of learning. He must be like the father of the family who loves all his children equally and simply accompanies them and supports them during their period of growth, setting an example WITH ASSERTIVENESS, DISCIPLINE AND LOVE.

When we reach this point of daring with just as much enthusiasm as our desire for self-improvement, regardless of the level one is at, we believe that everything is possible and that even the apparently craziest of dreams can come true. When we have a purpose, our first thought is that EVERYTHING IS POSSIBLE. If we truly wish for something deep down in our soul, the universe will expand our wish and it is very likely that it will become reality. Even if it is a whim, please make the most of the experience.

As a girl, I used to have certain breathing difficulties due to the bronchial asthma I suffered. On one particular occasion I was watching a film called *Marathon Man* starring Dustin Hoffman. The protagonist wanted to run in the New York marathon, and whilst I was lounging on the settee, short of breath, I promised myself: "One day I will run a marathon".

I actually experienced the film in my own flesh and bones, feeling that one day I would be able to do what the protagonist was doing. What is more, I managed to do just that in the pre-Olympic marathon of 1992 which I ran with so much joy inside me that I even jumped over the cones, to the horror of my trainer who considered that to be an unnecessary waste of energy. I achieved my goal. I overcame my asthma and breathing problems and managed to accomplish my mission. I thought to myself: "THE SKY'S THE LIMIT". THEN I REMOVED THE ROOF FROM THE SKY. NOW THERE ARE NO LIMITS. I NO LONGER LIMIT MYSELF.

Playing with the limits

The wonderful case of Olga comes to mind – she was a Zen student who proved to us how miracles can be worked, even on the verge of death. I remember how, at the end of the first day of the course, she approached me very short of breath and told me that she did not know whether she would be alive or not for the next day's class. According to the doctors, her illness was terminal and she was living on borrowed time. I asked her how she would feel if she was miraculously and completely cured. She admitted to this being the happiest thing that could happen to her at that moment. I told her: "Trust in yourself and tonight, before you go to sleep, practise conscious breathing and programme yourself to wake up in the morning. When you go to bed, programme yourself by telling yourself, 'Tomorrow I will wake up at such and such time'. With this order, you are commanding your body and your being to stay alive. This way, we'll see each other in class tomorrow. But first, let me give you a big hug full of life".

We joined in an embrace of unconditional love. The next day, in class, I asked: "Where's Olga?

When she raised her hand, I asked her: "So you're still alive then?

I publicly reminded her of the importance of giving thanks to the universe for the opportunity of being alive. She had terminal pancreatic cancer. With her permission, I started the class talking about her personal experience. I wanted the students to understand that you can choose to live if you are truly aware of life and of your power over it, and that even if you die by accident, even when you are dead, you can decide whether or not to return to life. You always have the choice.

Time went by and every day Olga would go to bed at night giving thanks for having lived another day, and programming herself to stay alive and wake up at the pre-established time. She felt better each day, so much so that she decided to have a blood test to find out what had changed in her body. In just one week she was surprised to learn of her complete and miraculous cure. Due to her experience, she discovered a new power, the power of life that is within each and every one of us. In her case, she had to come near to death in order to become aware of it. In fact, in our personal program there is always a final date which can never be exceeded, and when your time arrives, you will die, as your program allows no option for living any longer, although there is always the possibility of dying several times before reaching that final date.

IT IS SAID IN THE EAST THAT IF YOU WANT TO CHANGE YOUR LUCK IN LIFE, YOU SHOULD HAVE AN OPERATION OF SOME KIND. According to the people from the Far East, being under general anaesthetic is like experiencing temporary death, after which you return to life, as if you were resetting a computer. So, what is keeping you from having an operation on that bunion that has been bothering you for so long? This may be just the way for your luck to change, by altering your vibrational frequency. In fact, throughout our lives, we die many times, without being really aware of it; for example, if you have ever fainted or lost consciousness, whatever the reason may have been. You depart but come back in a second.

Ideally, we would have A CONSCIOUS DEATH. We should prepare ourselves for this transition, free of material, emotional and social attachments. We must be ready to come back to life and programme a new life. WE SHOULD DIE IN PEACE BY LIVING IN PEACE. This means resolving all our conflicts, ties and debts during our lifetime.

On odd occasions, even THE IMPOSSIBLE BECOMES POSSIBLE, in defiance of time and space and as proof that we are nothing. This happened to a couple of friends who were travelling by car. Suddenly, they came upon a lorry which was out of control and was about to crash into them head-on. They closed their eyes, expecting the worst, but the collision never occurred. Surprisingly, they found themselves on the other side of the lorry, driving in the same lane as before as if nothing had happened. The lorry had corrected its course. It was as if they had dematerialised one moment and materialised the next in a safe area, after an incredible quantum jump in time and space.

It is possible to consciously eliminate, as if it was a roll of film, an experience in your programme which has yet to be lived. If we stretch out the roll of film, we can locate the section of the experience which we want to erase and skip however many frames we prefer not to live through. We can edit the film, making the necessary cuts as we wish, thus eliminating the parts we would rather not experience. In this way, we consciously avoid having to undergo traumatic experiences, seeing as we have already learnt the lesson. Playing with time and space as if they were pieces of modelling clay is an experience of mastery.

A friend once told me that he made the most of a short spell in prison to practise meditation. During one profound meditation he completely forgot himself and when he opened his eyes, he found himself outside the cell. Fortunately, it was night-time and all was quiet in the corridors. He had to retrieve that total calmness through meditation in order to forget himself once more and return to his cell without attracting attention. He has discovered his ability to teletransport. If he had not been in prison, would he have had the opportunity to determine that ability?

*We can always change the perspective of things
if we study their symbols in depth.*

We can convert anything we deem negative into positive, making the most of the opportunities life offers us. If we believe that the number 666 is unlucky, we project that belief and create a similar vibration to what we think, attracting that experience to the present moment. For example, if you are travelling by car and all of a sudden you catch sight of a car number plate with the number 666, and this number makes you frightened, you run the risk of having an accident, given that you are creating this fear. Whatever we fear is exactly what we attract. If we convert the negative in positive and believe that 666 is $6 + 6 + 6 = 18$, which is the same as $1 + 8 = 9$, we get a positive number, seeing as 9 is the number of creation in women.

Therefore, we are able to convert all badness into goodness. This is called transmutation, which forms part of the mastery: being able to convert the negative into positive and to extract enriching experiences from difficult situations. This is the true meaning of the yin yang symbol.

Within the black area there is always a white spot and within the white area there is always a black spot. Within evil there is the seed of potential to create goodness, and vice versa. Within the experience of a conflictive situation, there is the potential to grow and learn.

Let me remind you that it is not the circumstances that are important but our attitude towards them. Do not forget the importance of our beliefs, of the creative power of our words and thoughts, of our inner strength when it comes to creating reality and experiences. Every day we must be more aware of what we feel, say, imagine and think, whatever the situation.

Mastery is nothing more than being able to attain this
state of total awareness, each and every moment,
in perfect equanimity and openness.

The beautiful thing about all this is that there is no such thing as a guilty person, a wicked or good person; there is just learning. In fact, 'up there', only our good deeds are noted. Our errors go unnoticed, which means there are no guilty parties, just unaware ones.

As Jesus said on the cross: "Father, forgive them, for they know not what they do".

Just as a father does not judge his son because he has not yet learnt how to walk, so we should not judge anyone for their acts. The father does not become angry because he knows that his son is not guilty but just learning to walk. It all forms part of the progress of life. Everything is perfect.

Forgiveness

I n the same way, we should not blame ourselves. And even though you put your hand on your heart and repeat the words 'my fault', this means that you are learning. If we do not impose expectations on ourselves, we understand how each of us finds his own path through learning; therefore, there is no reason to accuse anyone of anything and even less to lay the blame. If there is no blame, we could even go as far as to say that it is not necessary to forgive anyone.

If you want to forgive someone, forgive yourself, until you realise that you neither have anything to be blamed for. There is no blame and no-one at fault; just human beings who are more or less awake, more or less aware. But everything comes at the right moment. Everything is perfect. Even a master suffers, but through the understanding, acceptance, peace and happiness of knowing and proving that everything contains a lesson and a direction; due to illness, for example, as has been the case with many masters in the past. We are about to become a master or a Buddha, and as they say in the East, there are as many Buddhas on this planet as grains of sand in the River Ganges.

Buddhahood, enlightenment or awakening are all the same thing. This state is reached when one attains the frequency or state of peace and calm in mind, heart, body and spirit. It is precisely that point where a person manages to forget himself completely in a second and penetrate nothingness to find himself immersed in totality. Here he fuses with the light of unconditional love, filling his soul with bliss, joy or ecstasy. At that moment he knows that he forms part of the whole and feels 'at home'. From then on, nothing is the same. He has become his inner child once more; pure innocence. He understands the meaning of life. He knows that he has only to live life without a care in the world. His new light will act as a beacon for many who will follow him because they feel a special attraction without knowing the reason why. You too can be that beacon. IF I CAN, YOU CAN. *Dare to be your Master.*

The key to finding your inner peace

How can we live in peace?

If you have the opportunity to attend a Zen course, it will be of great help to you. The practice is based on the control of the central nervous system by means of conscious breathing, meditation and the Zen touch. It has nothing to do with any religion. You will find more information at:

http://suzannepowell.blogspot.com.es/2013/04/el-curso-zen-que-es.html.

Over the last years, several books and videos have particularly inspired me: *Initiation* by Elizabeth Haich; *The Four Agreements* by Miguel Ruiz; *Conversations with God* by Neale Donald; *Wake up to Life* by Anthony de Mello; *The Work* by Byron Katie; *The Mirror Rule* by Yoshinori Noguchi.

Whatever resonates with you forms part of your journey, your programme. If you are able to imagine an incident, regardless of how absurd and impossible it seems, it means that it forms part of your programme. Steer straight towards this idea with passion. Then add even more passion to your direction; without limits. The more enthusiastic you are, the sooner it will be manifest.

These are the tools and techniques that have worked for me, but everyone must find his own formula, books, masters, places and companions along the way. Each person must find his own path, programme, vision and inner purpose.

When you find something you are passionate about, your frequency is raised and you reach high rates of inspiration. This allows you disconnect from your mind; then, the information from your hard disk or super-memory is transmitted to your physical mind.

Here are some pearls of wisdom which might help you to reflect, behave and find that spot of light which you cherish inside you:

- Forgive, forget and accept.
- Live and let live
- Calm down and relax

- Be the eye of the hurricane. Stayed centred.
- Do not expect to change anyone.
- Write down your questions and concerns in a notebook.
- The answers and solutions will appear in dreams, meditations, books, through friends and wherever you least expect them.
- Open your eyes and ears. Pay attention to the signs.
- Observe everything with attention and maximum range of perspective.
- Pay attention to your co-creative words and thoughts.
- Do not blame anyone for your problems.
- All difficulties are just opportunities to leave your comfort zone and evolve.
- Give thanks to your masters; those who make you angry, drive you up the wall, put you on edge. They are like angels in disguise, who help you to see what is keeping you from attaining self-mastery. Observe your reactions in their presence.
- Abandon the reactive mode. Stop exhausting yourself, trying to defend anything.
- Be right or be happy? The decision is yours.
- In a conflictive situation, everyone is right, so acknowledge the fact, accept it and forget it.
- Laugh more and do not take everything so seriously.
- Re-invent yourself when you become bored or depressed. Creativity is born from boredom.
- Be prepared to suddenly change, whatever the situation.

- Do not take refuge in anything or anybody. Re-cal-culate. Adapt to all situations with acceptance and learn from them.
- Practise total non-attachment. The less you have to protect, the less your fear of losing it.
- Do not accumulate debts as these only deprive you of peace and forgive those who are indebted to you.
- Remember the Law of Correspondence: you will have whatever is due to you and whatever you need each moment to be happy, even though you may not be totally aware of it. It is just a matter of accepting and believing. If you cannot perceive things this way, take a look at those who are less fortunate.
- Be yourself with all the consequences.
- Do away with fear, which is the opposite of love.
- Make the most of each moment to help others without expecting anything in return. In any event, you will be helping yourself.
- Give to others precisely what you wish to receive in life. If you want love, give love. Fearlessly.
- The universe expands everything. Bear this in mind, in goodness and in evil.
- Love, respect and take care of your body. It is your temple.
- Surrender to your Self and aspire to the most uplifting evolution.
- Learn to be the captain of your ship rather than drift along.

- Let your heart lead you in your deeds rather than your mind. The heart is King and the mind is at its service. Not the other way round.
- Take sufficient rest. When you are tired, your temperament changes.
- Refrain from giving advice if not asked for it. In this way you will avoid hurting feelings and egos, and also stay clear of pride and arrogance.
- Be flexible with yourself and with others. You will thus be more approachable and people will be at ease in your presence.
- Do not entrust the power over your happiness to anyone. Adopt the phrase: "I am happy with you and without you".
- Find joy in the success and happiness of others, and you will thus attract the same for yourself.
- Always think well of those around you. If you think badly, your thoughts will alter your vibration, which the other person will perceive and return to you.
- If you think someone is defaming you, you are opening the door to that experience and inviting it into your life. In this way, it becomes a reality. Take a breath and send that person thoughts of love, so that they will think differently.
- Always think positively about your body. Your cells receive all your messages and transform according to your thoughts. Love yourself.
- Always look for balance in everything: equanimity. If you laugh a lot, you will also cry a lot sooner or later. Accept it as being necessary.

- Remember that everything is possible and that miracles exist. Do not limit your experiences with a limited mind.
- Go with the flow in life, using the principle of least effort. It is the easiest path.
- Do not try to be happy. Just be happy. Flowers do not try to grow, they just grow.
- Ask for help whenever you need it. Do not allow pride to stop you from asking. You are also helping the person who helps you to be happy. You are surely happy when someone asks for your help. When we ask for help, we become humble.
- Learn to say 'no' and express your true wishes. Do not abandon your path through being trapped in a situation which is not to your liking. Take the liberty of politely saying 'no'.
- Be spontaneous and happy like a child and try to spend time with children so as to learn how to recover your innocence.
- Do not impose your beliefs or theories on others. What is good for one may not be so for another.
- Everyone has their own particular gift to share in life with humanity. Look for yours or help others to find theirs and your gift will be revealed.
- Refrain from dramatising or entering into the dramas of others around you. The importance of an issue depends on the importance you give it.
- It is not the circumstances that are important, but your attitude towards them.

- Record your dreams in a notebook as soon as you wake up. Do it before your feet touch the floor to avoid the risk of forgetting them. Dreams provide us with answers, messages, solutions and ideas for life, helping us to put together the pieces of the jigsaw puzzle which forms our programme.
- Time reveals all. So there is no need to rush to prove anything. Go with the flow.
- Respect other people's pace in everything. Do not interfere with it or you will confuse matters.
- Be the kind of partner you wish to attract into your life.
- Remember that the only thing that is constant is change. Everything is impermanent.
- As Gandhi said: "Be the change that you wish to see in the world".
- Never think that you are too insignificant to create a great impact. We are all drops of water in the sea and together we are the ocean. Someone must make the first move. Dare to be that first person. Dare to be your own master so that you may inspire others to be theirs. Be yourself, be happy, relax and shine. Be.

Conclusions

Having said all this, how do we attain the wisdom of mastery, other than through knowledge or information that we amass? Or, in other words, how do we reach our hard disk? "I want to live in peace! But people won't leave me alone". How often have we uttered these words? To live in peace we first need our body to be free of pain and suffering. If your tooth aches, you are not at peace. For this reason, your priority is to attend to your physical body and its needs. When your body is healthy and balanced it is easier to achieve mental peace. WHEN YOU HAVE PEACE OF MIND, YOUR SPIRIT IS ALSO IN HARMONY. WISDOM IS UNATTAINABLE WHEN TRANQUILITY IS LACKING. IT IS IMPORTANT TO REMEMBER THAT WISDOM DOES NOT MEAN KNOWING EVERYHTING AT ONCE, BUT KNOWING WHAT YOU NEED TO KNOW AT THE MOMENT YOU NEED TO KNOW IT. THEREFORE, ALL YOU NEED ARE THE RESOURCES WHICH ARE NECESSARY TO MAINTAIN

YOUR INNER PEACE, CALM AND HARMONY IN WHATEVER THE CIRCUMSTANCE. THIS IS THE ART OF ZEN.

Whatever disturbs your mind provides an opportunity to be Zen. This is why we can say that life, God or the universe presents you with what you do not like so that you may learn to love it. Love is the most uplifting frequency.

When you reach the frequency of unconditional love, everything which is not on that frequency disappears from your reality.

When you awaken to life, you begin to love everything.

Therefore, to come into line with self-mastery, you must love life, love the planet and all its inhabitants and sentient beings. By doing this, you will love yourself. When you reach this frequency, you will have integrated your Self with your personality, or identity as a truly complete human being.

The path of self-mastery is learning to be a genuine person, that is to say, a complete person who has learnt how to integrate his Self with his physical person and how to fulfil himself as a true human being at the service of his Self. He simply Is.

Live as much as you want. To attain self-mastery you need not do anything. You just need to Be. People often tell me: "Phew, to achieve all that involves so much work. What must I do to be my own master?" I always answer the same thing: "You don't need to do anything". It is a matter of learning to not be anything, and not think anything in order to attain absolute nothingness, pass through it and hence arrive at being, the Whole. Go back along the path you have been following, detach yourself from everything and empty yourself of everything. Just be.

We are at the same time, very small yet very great. The physical body, compared with the universe, is nothing at all. Due to our ego and mind, we think that we know everything. So many qualifications, so much studying, so much amassed... and for what? When we say 'I', we always point to our chest and not our head. We are nothing, yet everything. The eternal part of us always is. But when we abandon the suit we have worn throughout this lifetime, it is reduced to dust. And the Self continues its journey, reprograms a new life and when it is reborn, puts on a new outfit.

During this lifetime, offer smiles to those angels who accompany you on your journey. Feel privileged to have the opportunity, as a Being, to live a physical, fair and fulfilling life. Just do it!

Thank you, thank you, thank you.

Thanks

Thanks to everyone, especially to you, Joanna, my eleven-year-old daughter, for showing me that I have not yet reached self-mastery. We all learn something from everyone. We are all masters and disciples.

Infinite thanks to Isabel and Elisabeth for their most generous help in the correction and adaptation of this channeling into text form.

Thanks also to Xavi for those four days he dedicated to carry out the transcription of the dictation of the channeling of this book, expressed in just fifteen hours during those days. "Just do it" always produces results. Mind out, action!

Information of interest

Suzanne Powell's Blog:
http://suzannepowell.blogspot.com.es/.

Facebook: https://www.facebook.com/pages/Suzanne-Powell/197392636971654.

Zen talks:
http://suzannepowell.blogspot.com.es/201304/po-nencias-zen-algunas-de-las-charlas-de.html.

Collective Reset:
http://suzannepowell.blogspot.com/2011/01/suzanne-powell-eñ-reset-colectivo-y-el.html.

Index